文物出版社

峨眉山
The Cultural Relics of 文
Mt. Emei 物

文物出版社

峨眉山文物
The Cultural Relics of Mt.Emei

编著：
峨眉山风景名胜区管理委员会
峨眉山旅游股份有限公司

学术顾问：
罗哲文　郭　旃
策划：
罗佳明　马元祝
编辑委员会
主任：
马元祝　秦福荣
主编：
王子今　冯庆川　高大伦
编委：
王子今　白云翔　孙家洲　罗佳明　马元祝
秦福荣　冯庆川　高大伦　傅　洪　罗声群
邹志明　陈黎清　曾德仁　黄剑华　杨荣新
徐　科　陈　耿　毛文筑　熊　锋　周　聪
主持单位：
峨眉山风景名胜区管理委员会
四川省文物考古研究院
鸣谢：
四川省文物管理局
故宫博物院
中国社会科学院考古研究所
中国秦汉史研究会
四川省历史学会
四川大学历史文化学院
四川师范大学巴蜀文化研究中心
四川省社会科学院历史研究所
成都博物院

峨眉山文物
The Cultural Relics of Mt. Emei

序 Preface

峨眉是我国最重要的名山之一，为天下之雄，被称为震旦第一山。本属蜀国、汉代属蜀郡南安县，后归犍为郡管辖。晋人常璩《华阳国志》的《蜀志》记载，南安县"南有峨眉山，山去县八十里。《孔子地图》言有仙药，汉武帝遣使者祭之，欲致其药，不能得"，可见当时峨眉已经由于富有神秘传说而受重视。

近半个多世纪以来，峨眉山及其周围地区的文物考古工作逐步开展，有一系列重要发现，使这里悠久的历史文化传承得以揭示，与峨眉秀美珍奇的自然景观相结合，吸引了国内外学术界、艺术界以及广大公众的密切关注。

黄湾大车坝出土的石器，见证了峨眉一带早在新石器时代已有先民繁衍生息。柏香林、石岗村、罗目镇等地点发现的青铜器、陶瓷器、石雕、钱币等等文物，更以物质文化遗产的形式，提供人们直观了解峨眉山历史的条件，与种种有关载籍文献互相印证。

大量文物证明，至少在战国时期峨眉已有高度的文明。符溪柏香林于巴蜀考古中有引人注目的地位，所出194件青铜器质地良好，工艺精美，有的还带有至今尚难解读的巴蜀文字。到汉代，当地的农业生产发达，石岗村的田塘模型是生动的反映。

佛教的传流为峨眉开辟了新的局面。北宋太平兴国五年（980年），太宗命人在成都铸造普贤菩萨铜像，运至峨眉，从此峨眉作为中国佛教四大名山之一的普贤道场，声名远播。寺庙文物，包括建筑、佛像、写经、书画等，均极珍贵。

古时蜀道难行，观览峨眉风光文物实非易事。明代学者陈第曾遍访五岳，著有《五岳游草》，最后发愿前往峨眉，竟卒于中途，终成遗憾。现在峨眉已成为国内外瞩目的世界文化与自然双遗产，第三届世界自然遗产会议将在这里召开，而精选峨眉文物的《峨眉山文物》一书也作为会议献礼出版。这充分表明，峨眉山人在新的历史时期中一定会不负众望，创造出新的辉煌。

李学勤

2007年9月16日于清华大学

The imposing Emei Mountain is reputed as the most majestic in China. Originally belonging to the Shu Kingdom, it was under the jurisdiction of Nan'an County of Shu in Han Dynasty and was later under the jurisdiction of Jianwei County. "Mount Emei towers in the south of Nan'an County, 80 li away from the county seat, where elixirs are treasured based on the *Atlas of Confucius' History*. *The Shu Chronicles* of the *Records of Huayang Kingdom* compiled by Chang Qu in Jin Dynasty records that, "Upon hearing the news of elixirs, Emperor Wu in Han Dynasty dispatched emissaries to pay homage to the mountain, intending to fetch the miraculous elixirs, but in vain". This clearly indicates that Emei Mountain already attracted much attention at that time with its rich and mysterious legends.

Since the recent half century, archaeological fieldwork has been gradually undertaken in Emei Mountain and its peripheral areas and results in a number of significant excavations disclosing its profound history and cultural deposits. Integrating with the natural beauty, the cultural relics here have aroused the concerns of academic and artistic communities as well as public interest.

The stone wares unearthed in Dacheba of Huangwan Township have witnessed the life of the ancient people in as early as the Neolithic Age. The bronze wares, chinawares, stone carvings, coins, and many other cultural relics excavated in Boxianglin, Shigang Village and Luomu Town have provide people a direct access to understand the history of Emei Mountain and confirmed corresponding records and documents related to it.

Large numbers of excavated cultural relics can well prove that Emei Mountain had experienced a booming civilization dating back to as early as the Warring States Period. Boxianglin in Fuxi, with a remarkable place in the archaeological study of Bashu Culture, has witnessed the excavation of 194 exquisite bronze wares, with some of which even bearing traits of the elusive Bashu Culture. Till the Han Dynasty, the local agriculture was very developed with the rice field and pond model found in Shigang Village as its vivid reflection.

The spread of Buddhism created a new situation for Emei Mountain. In the fifth year of Taipingxingguo of Northern Song Dynasty (980 A.D.), Emperor Taizong ordered his people to build a copper statue of Samantabhadra Bodhisattva and had it transported to Emei Mountain. Since then, Emei Mountain as the Bodhimandala of Samantabhadra has been reputed as one of the four famous Buddhist Mountains in China with a great treasure of precious monastery relics including architectures, Buddhist figures, scriptures, calligraphies and paintings, etc.

It is universally known that the roads to Shu had been really rough, and this created physical difficulties for people to view the beautiful scenes and cultural relics of Emei Mountain. Chen Di, a famous scholar in Ming Dynasty who had visited all the five famous mountains of China and composed the *Travelogue and Travel Notes of Five Sacred Mountains*, finally made a vow to reach Mount Emei, but failed unfortunately and was found dead halfway. Currently, Emei Mountain has become world natural and cultural heritage site. For this reason, the 3rd World Natural Heritage Conference will convene here. *The Cultural Relics of Mt. Emei* carefully compiled will be published as a gift to mark the holding of the Conference as well as a manifestation of the determination of the people of Emeishan City to live up to the hope of the general public to compose new glorious chapters in the new historical period.

Li Xueqin
Tsinghua University, Sept. 16, 2007

峨眉山文物

综述

巍巍大峨,从祖国四川西南地凸兀而起,雄秀天下。在过去漫长的历史岁月中,峨眉山不仅孕育了绮丽的自然风光,更遗存了大量珍贵文物,古蜀文明早已浸润到这块美丽的土地。"武王伐纣,实得巴蜀之师"(《尚书·牧誓》),当时古蜀国的疆界即以"玉垒、峨眉为城郭",悠久的历史既折射出古蜀文化的灿烂,更辉映着峨眉山迷人的文化内涵。本书所选列的文物,主要来自峨眉山博物馆。该馆现存文物共有4632件,其中三级以上(含三级)为1015件,这批文物地方性较强,绝大部分文物与峨眉山及其附近区域的重大历史发展阶段相关联,成为研究地方史的珍贵实物资料。大批的青铜器、瓷器、佛教造像、书画作品不仅具有历史、科学价值,而且有着较高的艺术价值。

寺庙建筑有着浓郁的川西南汉族山区村舍风格,与峨眉山自然环境融为一体,形成了点、线、面结合的山野寺庙园林群落体系,是"峨眉天下秀"的重要构成因素,故本书也精选了部分寺庙建筑及其附属文物供读者欣赏。

石器 石雕

1963~1988年,在沿青衣江(古羌江)水系的峨眉河流域的一、二级台地,东起峨眉城东郊1公里处的跃进渠和6公里处的柏香林附近,西至峨眉山景区内黄湾乡大车坝,东西相距约14公里,南北相距约5公里,纵横约40平方公里的范围内,先后采集、出土了一批石器。

这批石器的原料绝大部分采自当地的河床砾石,纵劈成片,由劈裂面与自然面同向打制而成。其形制均为双肩石器,与

雅安市、乐山市洪雅县止戈乡王华村、夹江县甘江镇二郎庙、迎江乡双龙村、云吟乡工农村以及乐山市中区安谷镇陈黄村等地出土的新石器基本一致。又与云南省云县芒怀新石器遗址的有肩石器属同一类型。故这批石器的时代，上限不超过新石器时代早期，下限可以晚到商周时期。

1977年11月，峨眉县双福镇石岗村农民取土制砖时发现一座砖室墓。此墓位于县城西北10公里，双福镇东4公里。现存有一直径约10米的封土丘，砖室墓穴在土丘西部，为长方形单室，长9.73米，宽2.23米，墓道长1.8米，宽1.7米。全墓均由花边砖砌成。墓门向南偏东10°，用单层砖封闭。砖侧花边纹饰有双凤对舞纹、菱形纹、联璧纹等。在四川地区已发掘的汉墓中，大多随葬陶俑，而出土石雕艺术品则相对较少。该墓出土了12件砂石圆雕明器，有田塘、执锸俑、听琴俑、蟾蜍、辟邪座等，是不可多得的艺术珍品。它们集中反映了当时农业的高度发达和社会安定，以及审美情趣。如田塘表现的是农业多种经营；辟邪则昂首怒吼，体态矫健，很有气势。正如鲁迅先生评价"惟汉人石刻，气魄深沉雄大"。

青铜器

青铜器数量之多、之精美，堪称峨眉山文物的一大亮点。1963年冬，峨眉县符溪镇新生村柏香林农民在平整土地时，于距地表0.7~0.8米深处挖出一批青铜器，到1980年柏香林墓葬群先后出土鍪、罍、戈、矛、斤、钺等青铜器194件，均具有鲜明的地方特色。本书选列的带盖铜鍪是最具代表的器物。铜鍪属饮器，在四川其他地区发现的几乎都没有盖，而这件铜鍪设盖，盖面饰阴刻变形虎纹一周，顶部有一豆形纽，上饰十字纹，雕刻精美，一虎首衔环以八节链与器肩部的绳索纹耳相连。此器为研究鍪的造型演变提供了实物资料，更是峨眉山先人为我们留下的艺术珍品。

还有一件人虎纹铜戈，极具研究、艺术价值。戈上铸有巴蜀符号一组，由人、虎组成，虎首在援末，怒目、竖耳、张口露齿，显得十分凶猛；虎身位于胡部，背阑腹刃，尾后曳，饰阴线虎纹。虎口下一人跪地，头接近虎口。似与西南地区少数民族中以人饲虎的风俗有关，在四川地区属首次发现，为研究古代巴蜀文化提供了重要的资料。

从广汉三星堆到金沙遗址，都发现有刻鱼纹的金器，而本书选列的鱼凫纹铜戈援上所饰鱼凫纹，头向锋，尾近圆穿，头略呈三角形，嘴上有一平置的带纹，端分歧垂于两侧，翼与两刃平行，末端芯尖饰雷纹，身饰鳞纹，尾左右分开呈燕尾状。疑为古代蜀人的族徽。

此外，书中选列的巴蜀文字铜戈、错银铜带钩及铜罍等，均为研究古代巴蜀文化的重要资料，也有较高的欣赏价值。

陶瓷器

1985年12月，在罗目镇的基建施工中，于距地表1米处发现一倒扣的陶缸。缸下铺一条形石板，板上重叠放置多件青铜器、瓷器和少量玉器。其中长颈瓶、凤耳瓶等属宋代的特有器形。

这批瓷器中的青白瓷盘碟均有芒口，其装烧工艺，系宋代大多采用器口着匣或器口着垫圈的复烧形式。瓷器中，绝大部

分是紫口铁足或足底呈铁锈红色，应是宋代名窑之一的龙泉窑烧制。龙泉窑采用的瓷土含铁质较多，并在烧成后受二次氧化，故有"紫口"和"锈红"出现。同时，瓷器的釉色、造型、烧制工艺，和四川境内的重庆、成都、温江、绵阳、郫县、阆中、广汉、德阳、大邑、广安、巴中、营山、武胜、青神、彭山等市县窖藏出土的同年代同产地的瓷器特征基本一致。

此外，还选列了峨眉山出土的几件宋三彩陶器。这些器物属低温釉陶器，泥胎表面用含铁、铜、钴、锰等元素的矿物作釉料着色剂，并加入很多铅作助熔剂，经低温烧制而成。釉色呈深绿、浅绿、蓝、黄、白、赭褐等多种色彩，实际上是一种多彩陶器，其用途主要用作随葬的明器。

书 画

峨眉山的馆藏文物中，名人书画几占其半。本书仅甄选出部分明末以来具有代表性的精品。

峨眉山书画以拥有一大批清代名人作品和近现代大师级作品而著称。峨眉山的声名在清代达到了又一高峰，当时全山寺庙有上百座，国内名人纷至沓来，文人骚客在这里吟诗作画，留下了大量的墨宝。如清代著名学者何绍基，在任四川学政时游览峨眉山，留下行书七字联"瓦屋寒堆春后雪，峨眉翠扫雨余天"，为峨眉山增色不少。何氏书宗颜真卿，取北魏碑版意趣，自成一体。

齐白石在1936年造访峨眉山，留下《墨芋图》。画作极是清新淡雅，款题："果玲大和尚清属，丙子夏五月，白石山翁齐璜。"钤朱文"白石"印，写于峨眉山报国寺待月山房。

曾任中央文史馆馆长的谢无量，也在峨眉山留下墨迹，"赵州言语示生路，临济宗风只活埋。百草千花相藉死，冰盆才见水仙开"。上题款"果玲上人指正"，下落款"无量"。其书法二王，吸取北碑的凝重散朗，天趣横生，自创一格。按其行止，应为1946年夏秋之际所作。

国画大师张大千在这里写有《秋荷图》，其画以水墨淡彩大写秋荷野鸳。画面上端题诗："一瓣真诚盖一鸳，西风卷地仅能掀。老枝力大争狮子，丈六如来踏不翻。"

郭沫若的行书"天下名山"横披，则是1959年9月应峨眉文物保护部门之邀书于北京。

此外，峨眉山博物馆征集有许多名人字画，如马琬水墨山水《□□雪霁图》、文徵明工笔彩绘《义勇武安王图》。其他还有曾国藩行书自题七字联、康有为行书自题七言诗轴（此轴1922年书于上海龙华寺，后由该寺僧元照携来峨眉山）等。本书还特别列选了多幅李琼久先生的作品，其善长山水花鸟、佛教人物，多取材于峨眉山，故有"李峨眉"之称。

佛教造像

学术界一般认为佛教传入中土大约是在东汉明帝时期，佛教的弘传离不开佛像，故古人亦称像教。在佛像传入的初始阶段，在四川乐山麻浩崖墓享堂横梁上刻有一尊手施无畏印的坐佛，其时代为蜀汉时期。其后在四川彭山、绵阳等地崖墓中出土了刻有原始仙佛的摇钱树座和摇钱树，说明四川自东汉以来佛教活动甚为兴盛。还有公元4世纪末僧慧持在观心坡下营造普贤寺（今万年寺）的传说。唐宋时期是四川佛教造像的黄金时代，有著名的乐山大佛、安岳卧佛、广元千佛崖、夹江千佛岩等精美造像。公元10世纪中叶，宋太祖赵匡胤派遣以僧继业为首的僧团去印度访问，继业回国后奉诏在峨嵋山营造佛寺，译经传法。宋太宗时遣使在成都铸造了重达62吨的巨型普贤铜像，供奉于今万年寺内，成为峨眉山佛像造像中的精品。至元明清时期，藏传佛教兴盛，本书收录有不少属于藏传佛教造像和尼泊尔风格的造像。

峨眉山的佛教造像多种多样，有玉佛、鎏金铜佛、木雕鎏金佛等。如书中列选的一尊佛教密宗造像——阿閦佛，是金刚界五智如来中的东方如来。按密宗教义，金刚界是体现大日如来"智德"的，共有五种智德，并为教化众生而化为五方五佛，其中东方阿閦佛就代表了大圆镜智，亦名金刚智。此像为整块缅甸玉雕凿而成，玉质柔美，弥足珍贵。又如一尊鎏金木雕佛像，外观具有铜像一般的质感。

峨眉山是普贤菩萨的道场，现存有众多的普贤铜像。书中列选的普贤菩萨骑象鎏金铜像，其形制是宋代以后佛教造像中的普遍做法，头戴镂空花冠，慈眉善目，披双领下垂式袈裟，胸前饰缨珞，单跏趺坐于六牙象上。《华严经》云："一切诸佛有长子，彼名号曰普贤尊。""佛之长子普贤菩萨，道证一尊，德圆两足，能圆众生所愿。"据《法华经》，普贤菩萨曾告诉佛，若有人颂读该经，"我尔时乘六牙白象王，与大菩萨具诣其所，而自现身，供养守护，安慰其心"。这尊铜像就生动地体现了这一说法，人物造型线条流畅，象作卧地状，通体鎏金。

总之，峨眉山佛教造像数量之多、艺术之精美都令人叹为观止。

杂 件

本书选列的玉器、象牙器、紫砂壶、鎏金铜塔、水晶杯等，有的出土于峨眉山地区的墓葬、窖藏，有的是传世品，虽然数量不是很多，但是代表了一个方面，反映了从宋代到上世纪40年代末这段时间峨眉山一带的民情风俗。明、清时期的玉雕作品，以其玉质之美，琢工之精，器形之丰，使用之广，都是前所未有的，并在很大程度上借鉴了绘画、雕刻的表现手法，吸取了传统的阳线、阴线、平凸、隐起、镂空、俏色、烧古等多种琢玉工艺，融会贯通，使作品达到了炉火纯青的艺术境界。如一件鱼形佩饰，玉质莹润，倍显活泼可爱：鱼阔体扁身，嘴微张，背鳍高凸，前鳍贴身，后鳍由两侧向上分开，尾扇形上翘呈游动状，腮部钻有小孔挂绳，雕刻细腻，栩栩如生。

牙角器在古代文物中虽然多属小器，但一器之微，往往穷工极巧，考工考史，源远流长。《礼记·玉藻》："笏，天子以球玉，诸侯以象，大夫以鱼须文竹，……"由此可见，古人在礼器的制作上，除了玉笏以外，象牙笏是仅次于玉笏的礼器。本书选列的象牙笏年代虽晚，但品相一流，极为珍贵。另一件清代象牙数珠观音，是民间艺人依据佛教密宗经典创造的观音菩萨像。其身穿交领袈裟，左手持念珠于膝，右手覆其上。按照佛教的说法，手持念珠诵经可消除魔障，增长功德。

紫砂壶在明中叶以后与江南文人雅士的饮茶有关，逐渐与诗词、书法、篆刻相兼一体，成为中国茶文化的组成部分。本书选列的紫砂提梁壶在形制、做工等方面都有独到之处。壶

为酱红色、椭圆形壶身、藤枝状提梁，梁前部分双枝塑于藤枝状曲流两侧的壶肩上，弧形盖，上有藤枝状纽，纽有孔，可穿绳与梁相系。

2002年，在峨眉山市罗目镇发现一座窖藏，出土了160多万枚宋代铁钱，其年号从北宋的"元祐"到南宋的"宝庆"等，计有17个，是我国同一地点出土铁钱最多的地方，对研究峨眉山周边当时的社会经济等有着重要的意义。值得关注的是，在这个窖藏中还出土了一件四川地区目前仅有的水晶杯，其材质好，制作精美，花瓣棱线分明，曲线流畅，堪称一流。

峨眉山人通过几十年、几代人的不懈努力，保护了大量珍贵文物，它们与山中的寺庙古建筑一道群星璀璨，光彩夺目，是峨眉山文化内涵的精髓所在。

寺庙建筑及其他

峨眉山现有寺庙27处。其中全国重点文物保护单位10处，四川省文物保护单位4处。从时代讲，除万年寺无梁砖殿为明代外，其余多是清代建筑。

峨眉山寺庙建筑的特点大致有如下几点：一是建筑格局因地制宜，依山就势，布置灵活多样，巧妙利用地形的高差，形成梯级升高的建筑格局，如伏虎寺、洪椿坪、雷音寺、清音阁等。其次，建筑多用木材，石料较少。三是没有中原地区那种官式建筑，未遵清《工部工程营造则例》的法式修建，没有彩绘作，少台梁式建筑，多为穿逗结构。四是具有民居性质，多为四合院落，世俗性倾向明显。最后，寺庙名多有来历，如伏虎寺，为南宋绍兴年间僧士性建尊胜幢，以镇虎患，故名。

报国寺是峨眉山著名寺庙，现为全国重点文物保护单位，是按四川民居建成的典型寺庙。清同治五年（1866年）扩建为五重殿宇的大寺，占地60亩。整个建筑均为木结构，复四合院组合，依地势、按中轴线逐级升高。主体建筑按山门、弥勒殿、大雄殿、七佛殿、藏经楼序列，四周建厢房为生活区，给僧人、信众营造出温馨祥和的环境。

值得注意的是万年寺无梁砖殿内的普贤铜像，是峨眉山最早被公布为全国重点文物保护单位。普贤铜像重达62吨，为北宋太平兴国五年（980年）建造。而砖殿属明代建筑，为单体布局，顶呈覆钵状，体近正方，石基、砖拱、无梁，堪称四川古建筑一绝。

清音阁（含牛心寺、广福寺）位于牛心岭下，2006年5月被统归为峨眉山古建筑群，为全国重点文物保护单位。其特点是寺庙园林与自然景观巧妙结合，构成一组风格独具的峨眉山寺庙园林建筑群体，体现了峨眉山寺庙园林的"幽"和"雅"，著名的"双桥清音"即是代表。

峨眉山寺庙文物的精巧要数洪椿坪寺中的千佛莲灯。灯体镂空，雕有佛道造像320尊。七个翘角为泥塑云龙神兽，以及《封神榜》所描述的道家故事人物，华丽无比，叹为观止。此灯为1928年来自重庆的工匠耗时3年制成。

峨眉山寺庙文物另一大特点是许多材料为铜质，除上述普贤铜像外，还有铜塔、铜佛像、铜观音像、铜钟、铜门等。

圣积寺铜塔原置于峨眉县城南的圣积寺内，以寺得名。又因塔体内外铸有《华严经》和佛像4700余尊，故又名华严宝塔。塔为紫铜铸造，其铸造年代据刘君泽《峨眉伽蓝记·圣积寺》，为"元时永川万华轩者所施造也"。

白龙洞寺内的南宋数珠观音铜坐像，过去一直被认为是铁质，直到近年对其维护时才发现为铜铸。此像头戴花冠，佩华丽璎珞，左手执念珠，右手置膝上，单跏趺坐，整个造像比例匀称，具有较高的艺术水平。

圣积寺铜钟，据钟体铭文及明大学士陈以勤著《别传禅师塔铭》记载，为明嘉靖甲子年（1564年）闰十二月二十四日铸造于四川古江阳郡（今泸州、富顺间），次年运至峨眉县郊虹溪桥打磨钻字。明隆庆丁卯年（1567年）八月十四日，悬挂于峨眉城南圣积寺。1982年在报国寺山门对面凤凰堡上建"圣积晚钟"亭，置于亭中。

金顶铜碑，现藏于峨眉山金顶华藏寺内。正面刻明翰林院检讨王毓宗撰《大峨山永明华藏寺新建铜殿记》，集晋王羲之书；背面刻中宪大夫、四川等处提刑按察司副使傅光宅撰《峨眉山普贤金殿碑》，集唐褚遂良书。

正是基于峨眉山所拥有的独特自然资源和深厚的文化内涵，1996年，联合国教科文组织公布峨眉山为世界文化与自然遗产。我们编撰此书的目的，就是要通过对这些珍贵文物的展示，触摸峨眉山深厚的文化底蕴。本书选列文物等照片160幅，按石器石雕、青铜器、陶瓷器、书画、佛教造像、杂件、寺庙建筑及其他七大类分章列序，均附有赏析文字，读者可从中领悟到峨眉山作为世界文化与自然双遗产所独有的魅力。

《峨眉山文物》编写组
2007年9月

The Cultural Relics of Mt. Emei
Introduction

Imposing Mt. Emei, famous in southwest China, charms the world with its unmatched beauty and majesty. In its long history, Mt. Emei has not only nurtured beautiful natural landscape, but also inherited a large quantity of rare and precious cultural relics. It is the place which had been nourished by the civilization of ancient Shu in the remote past. As is recorded in *The Speech at Muye in Shangshu*, "Emperor Wu (Zhou Dynasty) succeeded in the crusade against Emperor Zhou (despot of Shang Dynasty) because he obtained the brave armies of Ba and Shu". At that time, "Yulei (Jade Peak) and Mt. Emei served as the boundaries of ancient Shu Kingdom". The long history of Mt. Emei does not only reflect the splendor of ancient Shu culture, but also the profound cultural connotations of its own.

The cultural relics selected into this book are mainly from the Mt. Emei Museum. The museum has a collection of 4,632 pieces of cultural relics, including 1,015 ones above Class 3. These cultural relics bear great local characteristics and are mostly related to the major historical periods of Mt. Emei and its surrounding areas, serving as precious material objects for local history study. For example, the bronze wares, porcelain wares, Buddhist sculptures, paintings and calligraphic works are not only of historical and scientific value, but also of relatively high artistic value.

The temple architectures in Mt. Emei also possess typical western Sichuan style. They are delicately integrated with natural landscapes and form a system of mountain temple-garden clusters which are the major integral part of "Emei's elegance under heaven". Therefore, this book has carefully selected part of the temple architectures and the cultural relics preserved in them for readers to appreciate.

I

From 1963 to 1988, a large group of stone wares had been

excavated along the Grade I and Grade II terraces of the Emei River and Fuwenhe River valleys of the Qingyijiang River (ancient Qiangjiang River) system, in an area of 40 km^2 which is 14 km long from east to west and 5 km wide from north to south stretching from the Shimianyan Canal (1 km from the eastern outskirts of Emei City) to Baixianglin (6 km from the eastern outskirts of Emei City) in the east to Dacheba, Tianjing Township, Eshan Town in the Mt. Emei Scenic Area in the west. `The upper time limit of these stone wares is early Neolithic Period and the lower time limit is Shang and Zhou dynasties. The stone axe with shoulder included in the book is a representative artifact of these excavated stone wares.

The large quantity and exquisiteness of the bronze wares constitute a highlight of the cultural relics of Mt. Emei. In the winter of 1963, when the farmers of Baixianglin of Xinsheng Village in Fuxi Town of Emei County (today's Emeishan City) were leveling the land, they dug up a batch of bronze wares from 70-80cm underground. By 1980, 194 pieces of bronze wares had been excavated successively from the Baixianglin grave group, including *Mou* (drinking vessel), *Lei* (drinking vessel), *Ge* (dagger), *Mao* (spear), *Jin* (axe) and *Yue* (tomahawk) with distinctive local features. The bronze Mou with cover included in this book is the most representative one of these bronze wares. From the perspective of application, it falls into the category of drinking vessels. Such vessels have also been found in other places in Sichuan, but all without covers. The one mentioned above does not only have a cover, but also a circle of incised carving of decorative pattern of deformed tiger on the cover, providing new physical evidence for the study on the modeling and evolution of bronze Mou. Gracefully shaped, this Mou can be regarded as an artistic masterpiece left to us by ancient Emei people.

On 8 December 1985, in the course of the infrastructure construction in Luomu County in Emeishan City, from 1 meter underneath the land surface, was discovered an earthen jar in an upside-down position. Under the jar was a strip slate upon which were placed a lot of bronze wares, porcelain wares, and a few jade wares. Among them, the long-neck bottle and the vase with ornamental phoenix handles are products with unique vessel design of Song Dynasty.

In 2002, again in Luomu County, a cellar storage was discovered. Apart from the large quantity of iron coins, also unearthed were a group of porcelain wares of the same style. Of these porcelain wares, most striking was the shadowy celadon (also blue-white porcelain). Therefore, this book also includes the photos of two blue-white porcelain wares by courtesy of the Emeishan Cultural Relics Administration Office.

II

Nearly half of the collections of Emeishan are attractive paintings and calligraphic works of celebrities from the late Ming Dynasty to modern times. This book has only selected part of the most important collections which are precious cultural treasure of Mt. Emei as well as a highlight of the book.

Of the paintings and calligraphic works in Mt. Emei, many are works of celebrities in Qing Dynasty and modern masters. This has close relation to the spreading of the fame of Mt. Emei in Qing Dynasty when there were over a hundred temples in the mountain with domestic and overseas celebrities coming in a continuous stream and consequently a large number of calligraphic works of these scholars and poets have been left here. For example,

He Shaoji, an eminent scholar in Qing Dynasty, then a commissioner of education (Xuezheng) in Sichuan, when visiting Mt. Emei, left a seven-character couplet, "Wawu chilly with snow piles after spring, sky clean with Emei green after rain", which has added quite some charm to Mt. Emei.

In 1936, when visiting Mt. Emei, Qi Baishi left his painting "*Mo Yu Tu*"(dasheen in Chinese ink), which is of refreshing and elegant style. The autograph of the painting, "Painted by Mountain Old Man Baishi (Qi Huang) upon the kind request of Master Guo Ling in the summer of 1936", was written and the red-character seal of "Baishi" was stamped by Qi Baishi in the Daiyue Shanfang (Moon-waiting Mountain Abode) in Baoguo Monastery of Mt. Emei.

Xie Wuliang, the former curator of the Central Research Institute of Culture and History", also left his handwriting here, "The witty remarks of Zen Master Zhao Zhou unfold the path to enlightenment, while the tradition of Linji School is just to eradicate all worldly considerations. After hundreds and thousands of kleśas like rampant flowers and grasses wither successively, comes the turn of daffodil to blossom in glacial Mt. Emei." The preceding autograph reads "Humbly expecting the comments of Ven Guo Ling", followed by "Wuliang". Spontaneous and unique, the handwriting of Xie followed the styles of Wang Xizhi the father and Wang Xianzhi the son, and absorbed the dignified, elegant and unrestrained elements of the tablet inscriptions of Northern Dynasty This piece of work was made between the late summer and early autumn of 1946 according to his travel records.

Zhang Daqian, an accomplished master of traditional Chinese painting, also left here his painting Autumn Lotus, a freehand brushwork depicting in ink and light color the autumn lotus sheltering a wild mandarin duck. In the upper margin of the painting is a poem by Daqian, "A lotus leaf earnestly shelters a wild mandarin duck, even the strong west wind can not blow it apart. Its aged stem dwarfs a lion in strength, and easily withstands the golden body of Tathagatha."

The horizontal hanging scroll of "Tian Xia Ming Shan" (Famous Mountain under Heaven) in running handwriting was written by Guo Moruo in Beijing and then sent to Mt. Emei at the request of local cultural relic protection authority in September 1959.

This book also includes several works of Mr. Li Qiongjiu, a famous painter in Leshan and expert at landscape, flower and bird paintings, as well as Buddhist figure painting. As the themes of his paintings are mainly from Mt. Emei, thus he was given the appellation of "Li Emei".

Apart from the above-mentioned celebrities and their works, this book also includes some other masterpieces which we will leave to the readers to appreciate.

III

The academic circle generally maintains that the introduction of Buddhism into China approximately started in the reign of Emperor Ming of Eastern Han Dynasty. The spreading of Buddhism could not do without Buddhist images, so ancient people also called Buddhism the "religion of images". At the initial stage of the introduction of Buddhism into China, on the crossbeam of the ancestral hall of the cliff tomb in Mahao, Leshan City, Sichuan, was carved with a sitting Buddha with right hand in abhaya mudra, the gesture of protection or fearlessness. Afterwards, in the cliff tombs in Pengshan, Mianyang and other places in Sichuan, some money trees and tree seats carved with images of primitive immortals and Buddhas

were unearthed, indicating the flourishing activities of producing religious sculptures in Sichuan since the Eastern Han Dynasty. These activities might also have influenced Mt. Emei. Legend had it that in the 4th century, Monk Hui Chi built the Puxian Monastery (now Wannian Monastery) down the Guanxin (mind observing) Slope. Tang and Song Dynasties witnessed the golden times for the emerging of Buddhist sculptures. Among which, are famous and exquisite Leshan Giant Buddha, Anyue Sleeping Buddha, Guangyuan Thousand-Buddha Cliff, Jiajiang Thousand-Buddha Cliff, etc. In mid 10th century, Zhao Kuangyin, the first emperor of Song Dynasty, dispatched a delegation of monks led by Monk Ji Ye to visit India. When he returned, upon the imperial order, Monk Jie Ye came to Mt. Emei to build temples, translate Buddhist canons and spread the Dharma. He had people build a 62 ton huge copper statue of Samantabhadra Bodhisattva in Chengdu, which is now enshrined in the Wannian Monastery. This statue is not only a masterpiece of Buddhist statues in Mt. Emei, but also an unprecedented project in China's history of Buddhist art. In Yuan, Ming and Qing dynasties, the production of Buddhist statues marked the age of the thriving of Tibetan Buddhism and the decline of Chinese Buddhism. Among the Buddhist statues included in this book, there are statues of Chinese style, quite a number of Buddhist statues of Tibetan esoteric tradition and Nepalese style. These statues are mainly works of Ming and Qing Dynasties and have stood witness to the wax and wane of Buddhist art in China.

IV

The jade wares, ivory articles, purple gray teapots, gilded copper pagodas, crystal cups selected in this book are partly unearthed from the tombs and cellars in Mt. Emei and some of them are imperishable fine art crafts. Although these works are in small quantity, they are very unique and reflect the folk customs in the Mt. Emei area within a time span from Song Dynasty right down to the late 1940s. Ivory and horn articles are small items in ancient cultural relics, however, more often than not, in a tiny article, is infused with extremely exquisite craftsmanship handed down from ancient times. The *Jade-Bead Pendants of the Royal Cap* records that, "For his memorandum-tablet, the son of heaven used a piece of sonorous jade; the prince of a state, a piece of ivory; a great officer, a piece of bamboo, ornamented with fishbone." This serves as a proof that in ancient times, in terms of the production of ritual wares, apart from jade tablets, ivory tablets took the second place. The ivory tablets selected in this book, although are works of later periods, still remain quite precious due to their superior quality. Another ivory Guanyin (Avalokitesvara Bodhisattva) holding a string of beads in hand made in Qing Dynasty is a Guanyin statue created by folk artist according to the esoteric Buddhist canons. The Guanyin is dressed with a cross-collar cassock, holding the bead string in her left hand resting on the knee and covered by the right hand. According to Buddhist traditions, beads are not only used as counting device during the chanting of sutras, but also the means to eliminate evil obstructions and accumulate merits.

Purple gray wares are made of a special kind of china clay, Zini, or purple clay, at the temperature of 1150 degree C. The history of purple gray wares spans from Northern Song Dynasty to the present. After mid Ming Dynasty, purple gray wares were related with the tea ceremony of literati in the South of Yangtze River. Gradually, tea sets with the integration of teapot art, poetry, calligraphy, seal cutting emerged and became an integral part of China's tea culture.

The purple gray teapot with loop handle included in this book is remarkable in terms of its shape, workmanship, calligraphy and seal cutting. The teapot, reddish brown, oval-shaped, with vine-like loop handle, on whose front two twigs are molded along its shoulders, has an arc round lid with vine-like button with a hole through which the lid can be connected with the handle by thin thread.

In 2002, in the Luomu County of Emeishan City, a cellar was unearthed with storage of over 1.6 million pieces of iron coins of Song Dynasty, with 17 era names ranging from the Yuanyou Period in Northern Song Dynasty to Baoqing Period in Southern Song Dynasty. This place is the site in China where the largest number of iron coins has been unearthed and are of great importance for the research on the social economy of the regions around Mt. Emei then. For this reason, we have also included it in the book. One remarkable thing is that in the same cellar was also unearthed a precious coffee-colored six-petal crystal cup, which is the only one of its kind in Sichuan. Its material, exquisite workmanship, distinctive lines of the petals and smooth curves are all first-rate.

V

Mt. Emei currently has 27 temples including 9 national key cultural relic protection units (jointly called the Ancient Architecture Complex in Mt. Emei) and 4 Sichuan provincial cultural relic protection units. In terms of the historical periods of the buildings, apart from the Beamless Brick Hall of Wannian Monastery, the rest had mostly been built after Qing Dynasty. The temple architectures in Mt. Emei bear several characteristics. First, the layout of the architecture flexibly made use of the natural terrain of the mountain. Most of the architectures did not use brick and stone bases. Instead, they utilized the elevation difference and then were reinforced with stones on the ridges. A gradient development of these architectures had thus taken shape well represented by Fuhu (Tiger Subduing) Monastery, Hongchunping, Leiyin Monastery, Qingying Pavilion, etc. Second, these temples used much wood and less stone. Third, unlike the official architecture in Central and Northern China, they were not built in the Fashi (style) as regulated by the *Gongchen Yingzao Zeli* (The Imperial Specification for Buildings), without color painting, few in post and lintel structure while most in crossing beam structure Fourth, the characteristics of folk residences. The courtyard houses, mostly surrounded by trees, bearing apparent secular traits, are more suitable for secular residences, whereas their religious functions have been placed in a secondary position. Last, most of the names of the temples have their respective origins. For instance, the Fuhu (Tiger Subduing) Monastery, which was built by Shi Xing, a traveling monk in Shaoxing Period in the Southern Song Dynasty, for the purpose of subduing the tiger disaster, thus the name.

The famous Baoguo Monastery is a national key cultural relic protection unit which is also a monastery built in typical style of Sichuan folk residence. In the 5th year of Tongzhi Period (1866), it was expanded into a 60 mu large monastery with five layers of halls. Adopting wooden structure, the whole monastery is compound courtyard architecture with graded topographic elevation along the central axis. The main body of the architecture follows the sequence of Mountain Gate, Maitreya Hall, Sakyamuni Hall, Seven-Buddha Hall, Tripitaka Pavilion with surrounding wing-rooms as living quarters, creating a peaceful and tranquil environment for monks and Buddhists.

Quite noticeably are the beamless brick hall and the copper

statue of Pu Xian (Samantabhadra) Bodhisattva in Wannian Monastery, which is the first in Mt. Emei announced as a national key cultural relic protection unit. Weighing 62 tons, the copper statue of Samantabhadra Bodhisattva in the Beamless Brick Hall was built in the 5th year of Taiping Xingguo Period (980) in Northern Song Dynasty. Built in Ming Dynasty, the brick hall is a single structure building with its top resembling an upside-down bowl in quasi-rectangular shape. With stone base, brick arch, and no beams, the hall is indeed a marvel of ancient architecture in Sichuan.

Qingyin Pavilion (incl. Niuxin Monastery and Guangfu Monastery) sits at the foot of Niuxin Mountain. In May 2006, it was included into the ancient architecture complex of Mt. Emei and listed as a national key cultural relic protection unit. The remarkable characteristic of the pavilion is its artistic integration of temple gardens with the natural sceneries. The pavilion and the Heilongjiang Plank Way and Baiyun Gorge form a unique temple garden complex in Mt. Emei featuring tranquility and elegance, with the Double-Bridge Qingyin Pavilion as one of the representative buildings.

Another major feature of the cultural relics in Mt. Emei is that most of them are made of copper. Apart from the above-mentioned copper statue of Samantabhadra Bodhisattva, there are also copper pagoda, copper Buddha statue, copper Guanyin statue, copper bell and copper gate. It was right based on the unique natural resources and profound cultural connotations of Mt. Emei that on 6 December 1996 the UNESCO announced Mt. Emei as World Cultural & Natural Heritage. We have compiled this book in an effort to help the readers have close contact with the profound culture of Mt. Emei through presentation of these precious cultural relics. This book has selected 160 photos of cultural relics accompanied with over 20,000-character beautifully written descriptive texts and 11 sketches and is classified into seven major chapters i.e. stone wares (sculptures), bronze wares, porcelain wares (pottery), calligraphic works and paintings, Buddhist statues, miscellaneous articles, temple architectures and attached cultural relics. Each item of cultural relic has explanatory text from which readers can appreciate the unique charm of Mt. Emei as World Cultural & Natural Heritage.

The Compilation Group of
The Cultural Relics of Mt. Emei
Sept. 2007

峨眉山文物
The Cultural Relics of Mt. Emei

目录
Contents

序 李学勤
Preface by Li Xueqin

综述 《峨眉山文物》编写组
Introduction Editing Group of The Cultural Relics of Mt. Emei

石器\石雕　　024-033
Stone Wares \ Stone Carving

矛　Spear
镞　Arrowhead
有肩斧　Stone axe with shoulder
听琴俑　Music Listening Figure
执锸俑　Spade holding Figure
蟾蜍　Toad
辟邪　Talisman
田塘　Rice field & pond

青铜器　　034-061
Bronze Wares

敦　Frusta
四环纽蟠龙涡纹罍　4-ring Lei with volute dragon pattern
带盖单耳鍪　Single-handle Mou with ear
兽面纹三角援戈　Three-edge dagger with beast face
兽面纹三角援戈　Three-edge dagger with beast face
燕尾鸟纹三角援戈　Three-edge dagger with swallow-tail bird
人虎纹戈　Dagger with figure and tiger pattern
中胡戈　Medium minority dagger
鸟纹长援戈　Long dagger with bird pattern
虎纹中胡戈　Medium minority dagger with tiger pattern
龙纹中胡戈　Medium minority dagger with dragon pattern
凸穿十字形戈　Convex mounting cross-shape dagger

十字形戈	Cross-shape dagger
巴蜀文字戈	Dagger with Bashu characters
龙纹短骸宽叶矛	Broad spear with dragon patter
虎纹宽叶矛	Broad spear with tiger pattern
猎鹿纹宽叶矛	Broad spear with deer-hunting pattern
鱼凫纹宽叶矛	Broad spear with Yuhu pattern
人虎纹宽叶矛	Broad spear with figure & tiger pattern
长骸三穿双耳矛	Long-neck double-ear spear
无耳中骸矛	Earless medium-neck spear
楚式剑	Chu-style sword
扁茎剑	Flat narrow sword
虎斑纹柳叶剑	Willow-leaf sword with dotted tiger pattern
虎纹柳叶剑	Willow-leaf sword with tiger pattern
斧	Axe
斧	Axe
鱼凫纹斤	Jin with Yuhu pattern
平肩圆刃钺	Flat shoulder round hole yue

陶瓷器　　062-089
Porcelain Wares

三彩青龙　Three color blue dragon
三彩玄武　Three color Xuanwu
青白釉卷草纹碟
Blue & white porcelain dish of rolled-grass pattern
青白釉葵口碟 Blue & white porcelain dish
青花瓷盘　Blue & white porcelain dish
豆青瓷碟　Bean green porcelain dish
豆青瓷豆　Bean green porcelain bowl
影青瓷碟　Shadowy blue porcelain dish
豆青瓷碗　Bean green porcelain bowl

绛色开片瓷碗 *Deep red porcelain bowl*
白釉彩花碗 *White glazed color bowl*
绿釉莲花碗 *Green glazed lotus bowl*
瓜棱罐 *Melon-shape pot*
青花瓷罐 *Blue & white porcelain pot*
青花瓷杯 *Blue & white porcelain mug*
影青方口小瓶 *Shadowy blue square-mouth vase*
青花双耳瓷瓶 *Blue double-handle vase*
青白釉开片瓷花瓶 *Blue & white porcelain vase*
五彩仙翁瓶 *Five-colour god vase*
青花鱼缸 *Blue & white porcelain fish tank*
三彩陶凳 *Three-colour ceramic stool*

书画 090-135
Painting and Calligraphy Works of Famous Artists

□□雪霁图 马琬 *Sunshine after Snow by Ma Wan*
义勇武安王图 文徵明 *Brave Wu'an Prince by Wen Zhenming*
紫竹观音 竹禅 *Bamboo & Guanyin by Zhu Chan*
八哥图 徐悲鸿 *Birds by Xu Beihong*
高士观松图 张大千 *Pine Viewing by Zhang Daqian*
秋荷图 张大千 *Autumn Lotus by Zang Daqian*
墨芋图 齐白石 *Mo Yu Tu by Qi Baishi*
峨眉山水 黄君璧 *Mt. Emei Scnery by Huang Junbi*
芦雁图 吴青霞 *Swallow by Wu Qingxia*
佛教人物画 潘絜滋 *Buddhist Figures by Pan Jiezi*
玄奘法师像 潘絜滋 *Picture of Rabbi Xuanzang by Pan Jiezi*
红梅图 关山月 *Red Plum by Guan Shanyue*
香溢宇宙 李苦禅 *Fragrance Allover by Li Kuchan*
猫头鹰 黄永玉 *Owl by Huang Yongyu*
荷花 黄胄 *Lotus by Huang Zhou*

天女散花　程十发　*Fairy Maiden & Flowers* by Cheng Shifa
峨眉山色　李琼玖　*Emei Mountain* by Li Qiongjiu
珙桐白鹇图　李琼玖　*Gong Tong Bai Xian Tu* by Li Qiongjiu
峨眉山金顶　李琼玖　*Jinding of Mt. Emei* by Li Qiongjiu
峨眉山水　李琼玖　*Mt. Emei Scenery* by Li Qiongjiu
證知和尚肖像图　宝光　*Monk Zhengzhi* by Bao Guang
万壑一钟　松涛　*Wan Hu Yi Zhong* by Song Tao
行书　破山明　*Running script* by Po Shanming
行书　爱新觉罗·玄烨　*Running script* by Xuan Ye
行书对联　张船山　*Couplet in running script* by Zhang Chuanshan
隶书对联　陈鸿寿　*Couplet in Lishu Script* by Chen Hongshou
行书对联　何绍基　*Couplet in running script* by He Shaoji
行书对联　曾国藩　*Couplet in running script* by Zeng Guofan
行书　康有为　*Running script* by Kang Youwei
左书对联　廖平　*Couplet of left-script* by Liao Ping
行书　刘光第　*Running script* by Liu Guangdi
行书自题七绝诗　赵熙
Four-line Poem in Running Script by Zhao Xi
天下名山　郭沫若
Famous Mountain under Heaven by Guo Moruo
行书　谢无量　*Running script* by Xie Wuliang
行书自题七绝诗　何鲁
Four-line Poem in Running Script by He Lu
行书对联　刘梦伉　*Couplet in running script* by Liu Mengkang
行书对联　林散之　*Couplet in running script* by Lin Sanzhi

佛教造像
Buddhism Statues

136-159

灵山铜佛　　Lingshan Copper Buddha

鎏金释迦牟尼铜立像
Gilded Standing Copper Statue of Sakyamuni

鎏金释迦牟尼铜坐像
Gilded Sitting Copper Statue of Sakyamuni

鎏金释迦牟尼铜坐像
Gilded Sitting Copper Statue of Sakyamuni

鎏金释迦牟尼铜坐像
Gilded Sitting Copper Statue of Sakyamuni

鎏金释迦牟尼铜坐像
Gilded Sitting Copper Statue of Sakyamuni

鎏金普贤菩萨铜坐像
Gilded Sitting Copper Statue of Samantabhadra Bodhisattva

鎏金药师佛铜坐像
Gilded Sitting Copper Statue of Medicine Buddha

鎏金释迦牟尼铜坐像
Gilded Sitting Copper Statue of Sakyamuni

鎏金观世音铜坐像
Gilded Sitting Copper Statue of Avalokiteshvara Bodhisattva

鎏金观世音铜坐像
Gilded Sitting Copper Statue of Avalokiteshvara Bodhisattva

鎏金释迦牟尼、多宝佛并坐铜像
Gilded Side-by-Side Sitting Copper Statues of Sakyamuni and Many-Jewels Buddha

鎏金阿弥陀佛铜立像
Gilded Standing Copper Statue of Amitabha Buddha

鎏金阿弥陀佛铜立像
Gilded Standing Copper Statue of Amitabha Buddha

鎏金莲花观音铜坐像
Gilded Sitting Copper Statue of Avalokiteshvara Bodhisattva with Lotus

鎏金木雕大势至菩萨像
Gilded Wood-carved Statue of Mahasthamaprapta Bodhisattva

鎏金阿阁玉佛坐像
Gilded Sitting Jade Statue of Aksobhya Buddha

杂件　　　　　　　　　　　　160-177
Miscellaneous

错金银铜带钩　Gold & Silver Decorated Copper Belt

铜纺锤　Copper spindle

水晶杯　Crystal cup

铁钱　Iron coin

犀牛望月铜镜座
Copper Mirror Seat of Rhinoceros Viewing the Moon

鎏金铜塔　Gilded copper pagoda

象牙笏　Ivory Tablet

玉鲤鱼　Jade Cyprinus Carpio

翡翠环（扳指）　Sapphire ring (Banzhi)

象牙数珠观音像　Guanyin Statue Holding Ivory Beads

贝叶经　Beiye Scripture

寿山石洗　Shoushan Stonewash

紫砂壶　Purple Gray Tea Pot

银塔　Silver Pagoda

寺庙建筑及其他
Monasteries and Others   178-219

飞来殿 *Feilai Hall*

报国寺 *Baoguo Monastery*

伏虎寺 *Fuhu Monastery*

清音阁 *Qingyin Pavilion*

万年寺 *Wannian Monastery*

无梁砖殿 *Beamless Brick Hall*

纯阳殿 *Chunyang Hall*

神水阁 *Shenshui Pavilion*

洗象池 *Xixiang (Elephant washing) Pond*

金顶 *Jinding*

金殿 *Golden Hall*

华藏寺 *Huazang Monastery*

卧云庵 *Woyun Nunnery*

仙峰寺 *Xianfeng Monastery*

洪椿坪 *Hongchunping*

卢舍那瓷佛像 *Porcelain Figure of Vairochana Buddha*

数珠观音铜坐像 *Ivory Guanyin Holding Beads*

普贤铜像 *Copper Statue of Puxian*

铜三身佛像 *Three-body Copper Buddha Statue*

鎏金十方普贤铜像
Ten-heads Copper Statue of Puxian Buddha

普贤铜像 *Copper Statue of Puxian*

圣积寺铜钟 *Copper Bell of Shengji Monastery*

铜鼎 *Copper Tripod*

华严铜塔 *Huayan Copper Pagoda*

金顶铜碑 *Jinding Copper Tablet*

金顶铜门 *Jinding Copper Door*

第一山亭 *No.1 Mount Pavilion*	
摩崖石刻 *Cliff Carving*	
智者大师衣钵塔 *Clothing Pagoda of Master Wisdom*	
普贤愿王金印 *Golden Chop of Puxian*	
佛牙 *Buddha Tooth*	
第一山碑 *No.1 Mountain Tablet*	
千佛莲灯 *Thousand-Buddha Lotus Lamp*	
仙圭石 *Xian Gui Stone*	

附录　　　　　　　　　　　　　　　　220-227
Attachments
　　峨眉山古迹分布图 *Distribution of Historic Relics in Mt. Emei*
　　峨眉山大事记 *Chronicle Events of Mt. Emei*

后记　　　　　　　　　　　　　　　　228-229
Postscript

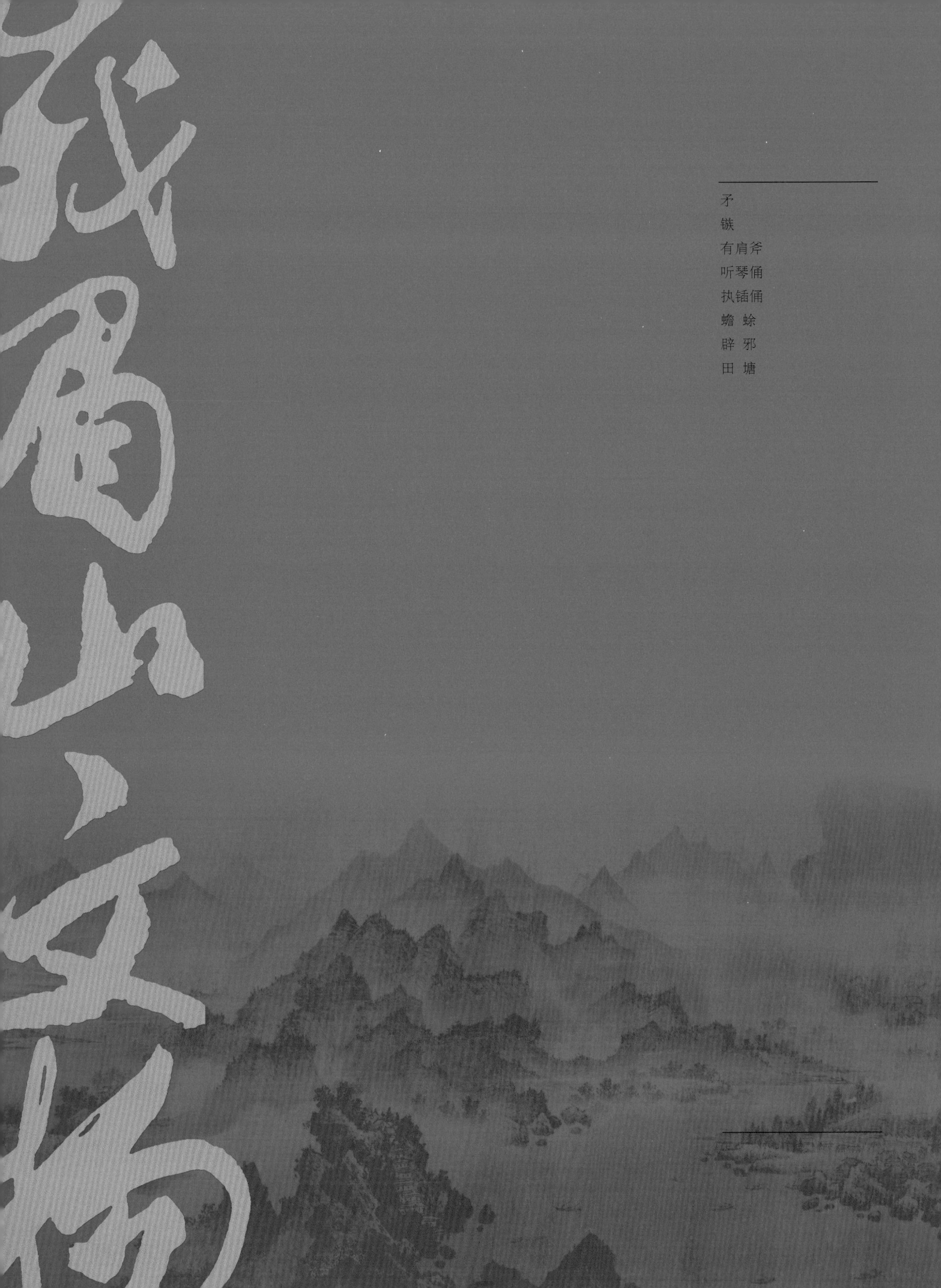

矛
镞
有　肩斧
听　琴俑
执　锸俑
蟾　蜍
辟　邪
田　塘

峨眉山文物

石器\石雕
Stone Wares\Stone Carving

024-033

矛
Spear

新石器时代（约1万年～4千年前）
通高6.8厘米
峨眉山博物馆藏
石质坳黑、三棱形、矛尖残、有使用的痕迹。

镞
Arrowhead

新石器时代（约1万年～4千年前）
通高8.3厘米
峨眉山博物馆藏
翼、铤分界明显、身截面呈菱形，有明显的使用痕迹。

有肩斧
Stone axe with shoulder

新石器时代（约1万年～4千年前）
通高15.3厘米
峨眉山博物馆藏
石英砂岩质，打制后又加以磨制而成。半圆形铲身、宽肩，柄两侧有明显的打击凹痕，刃弧形，下部有打制痕迹、左肩部略残。

Stone Wares \ Stone Carving
027

听琴俑
Music Listening Figure

东汉（25～220年）
通高54.5厘米
峨眉山博物馆藏
东汉晚期墓葬出土。为男性，头束发髻，身着右衽长衣，腰束带，席地而坐。左手扶膝，右手作掩耳状，面部表情专注，略带微笑，正在全神贯注地聆听琴声。

执锸俑
Spade holding Figure

东汉（25～220年）
通高68厘米
峨眉山博物馆藏
东汉晚期墓葬出土。为男性，头戴圆形小帽，圆脸、高鼻、两眼平视、口微张，身着右衽长衣、腰间束带、窄袖挽口，左手持锸，右臂侧举，右手残。整个造型既有纹饰的粗犷，又有表情的细腻，显得生动而又传神。

蟾蜍
Toad

东汉（25~220年）
通高37厘米
峨眉山博物馆藏
东汉晚期墓葬出土。立于方形座上。阔嘴，双目仰视，昂首，鼓腹，四腿弯曲，做向前跳跃状。身上有凸起的疙瘩，纹路清晰。背中部有边长4厘米的方孔，应是摇钱树的底座。

辟邪
Talisman

东汉（25~220年）
通高35.3厘米
峨眉山博物馆藏
东汉晚期墓葬出土。挺胸昂首，盘卧于圆形座上。头上双角，背有两翼及方形榫眼。身下饰云气纹。造型古朴生动，雕刻技法洗练，风格粗犷而又传神，是研究东汉石雕的珍贵资料。

Stone Wares\Stone Carving
031

田 塘
Rice field & pond

东汉（25~220年）
长61厘米 宽49厘米
峨眉山博物馆藏

四周为堤岸，田以埂分作两块，一块中刻有椎形小堆，似模拟粪肥堆积；另一块中有两人弓背插秧。塘与田、田与田之间均有进出水口，似为灌溉系统。塘的进水口处有一小池，似作澄积坭沙和灌调之用。池口拦有鱼篓。塘中种莲、有鸭两只，其一正吞食一鳅；有蟹一只、其爪正钳一鱼之尾；有蛙、鳖各一；有一小舟穿游其中。构思巧妙、雕刻技法娴熟。

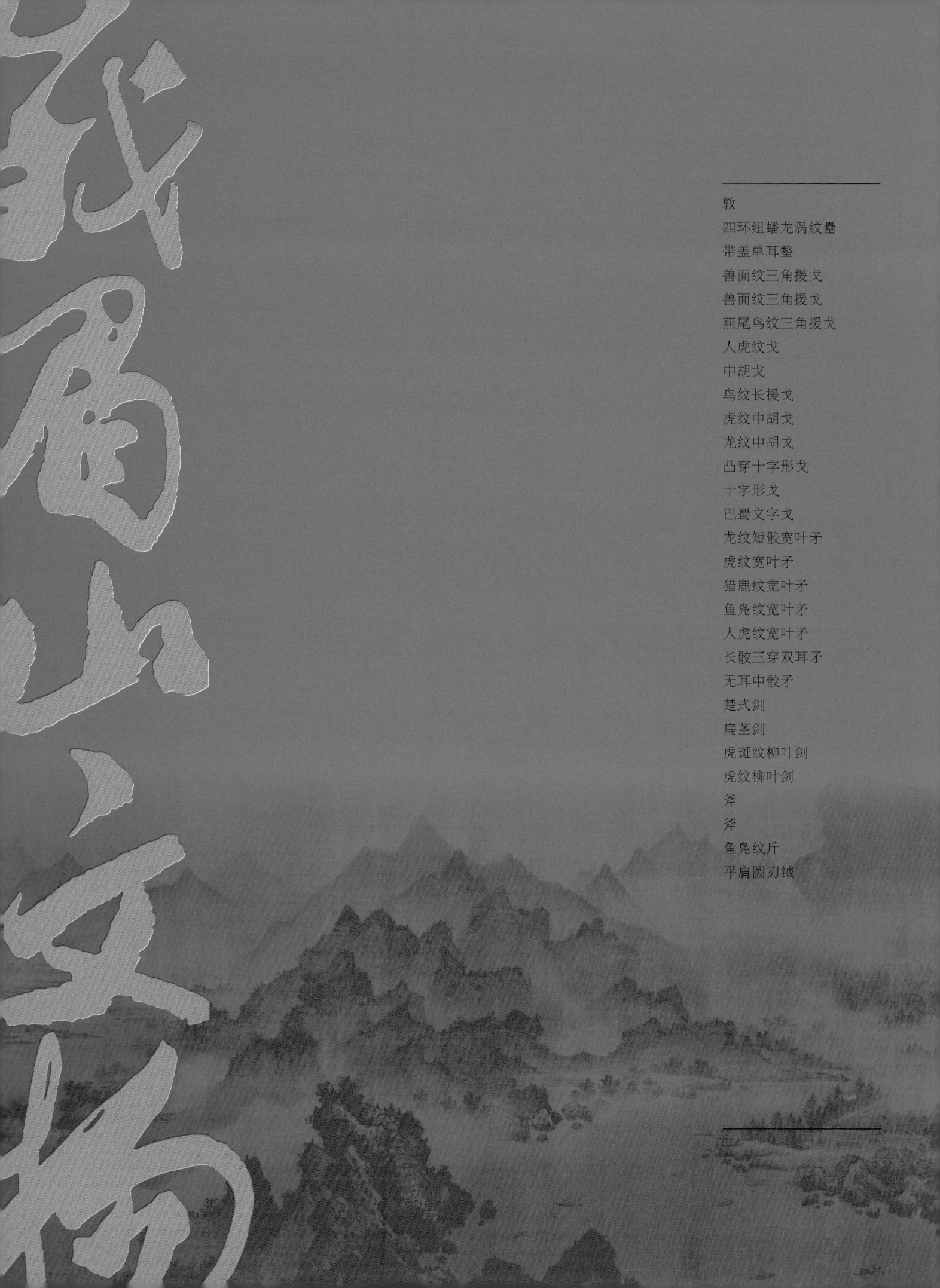

敦
四环纽蟠龙涡纹罍
带盖单耳鍪
兽面纹三角援戈
兽面纹三角援戈
燕尾鸟纹三角援戈
人虎纹戈
中胡戈
鸟纹长援戈
虎纹中胡戈
龙纹中胡戈
凸穿十字形戈
十字形戈
巴蜀文字戈
龙纹短骹宽叶矛
虎纹宽叶矛
猎鹿纹宽叶矛
鱼凫纹宽叶矛
人虎纹宽叶矛
长骹三穿双耳矛
无耳中骹矛
楚式剑
扁茎剑
虎斑纹柳叶剑
虎纹柳叶剑
斧
斧
鱼凫纹斤
平肩圆刃钺

峨眉山文物

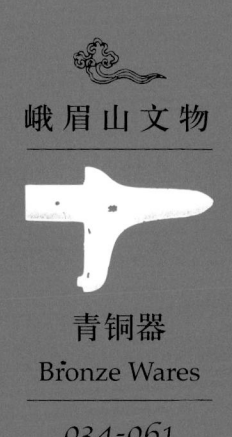

青铜器
Bronze Wares

034-061

敦
Frusta
战国（前475年～前221年）
通高24.8厘米
峨眉山博物馆藏
盖与器身形制、大小相同，相合近球形。盖上有三扁体虎形饰纽及双环耳，器侧环耳与盖耳相对应，三蹄形足。

四环纽蟠龙涡纹罍
4-ring Lei with volute dragon pattern
战国中晚期（前475年～前221年）
通高44.5厘米
峨眉山博物馆藏
四环纽盖，沿上有三个鼓突的兽形小铺首。器身方唇、鼓腹、斜肩、圈足。腹上部有四环形耳，环形耳间饰四蟠龙涡纹、颈肩饰云纹、勾连纹。此器涡纹内饰蟠龙，创意新颖。

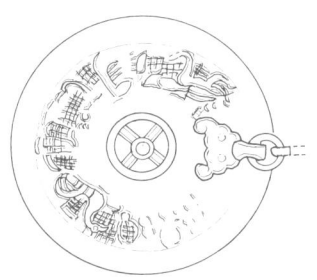

带盖单耳鍪
Single-handle *Mou* with ear

战国（前475年～前221年）
通高15.1厘米
峨眉山博物馆藏

侈口、束颈、鼓腹、圆底。通体素面，肩有绚纹环形单耳与盖连接。盖若覆盘，中间稍凸、扣形圆纽。纽上阴刻十字纹，近盖边缘处饰一周回纹与连珠纹组成的图案，其间刻有巴蜀图语。这种铜鍪极具战国蜀文化特色，为研究鍪的演变提供了重要的实物资料。

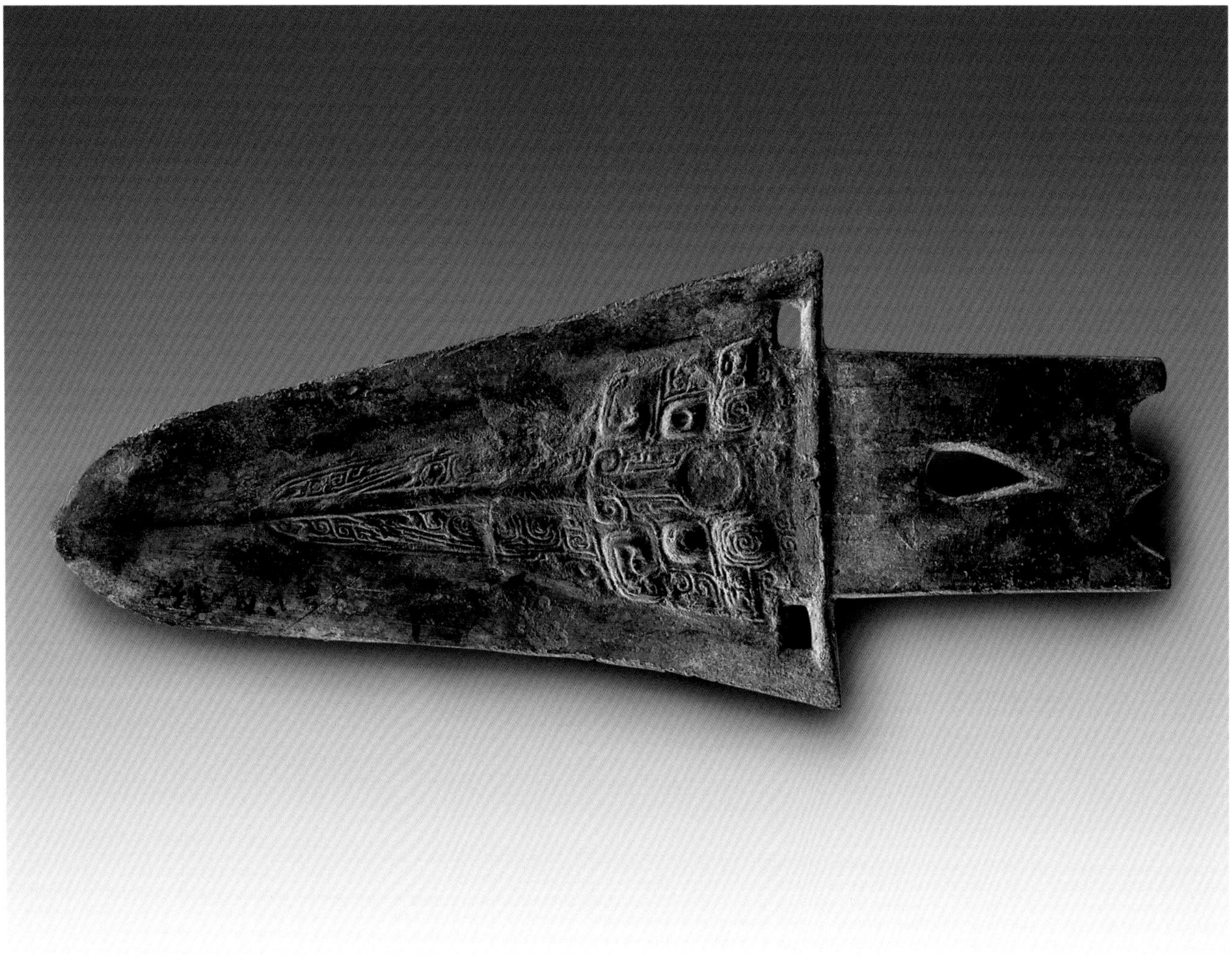

兽面纹三角援戈
Three-edge dagger with beast face

战国（前475年～前221年）
通长16.8厘米
峨眉山博物馆藏

三角形援，中有突脊，二穿。内上有心形穿，端作山字形。援本饰浅浮雕兽面及云纹。内部素面。

兽面纹三角援戈
Three-edge dagger with beast face

战国（前475年～前221年）
通长17厘米
峨眉山博物馆藏

三角形援，中有凸脊，近本处有一圆孔，二穿无胡，内上有橄榄形穿，端作山字形。援本饰兽面、其前有叶形云纹及暗斑纹，内端与穿之间饰浅浮雕巴蜀图语。

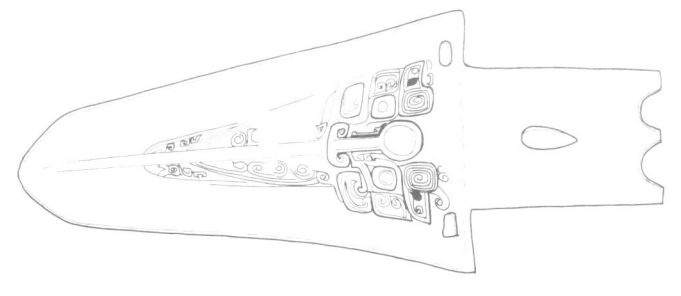

燕尾鸟纹三角援戈
Three-edge dagger with swallow-tail bird

战国（前475年～前221年）
通长18.6厘米
峨眉山博物馆藏

三角形援略内弧，近阑处有二条形穿，近本部有一圆穿，其上浮雕一站立羽人，张开羽翼。其下为浅浮雕燕尾状，头向锋，尾近圆穿。羽人头部似猫头鹰，嘴衔一平置蒂纹，两端弯曲分叉垂于两侧，双翼与两刃平行。末端芯尖饰云雷纹，身饰鳞片，双尾左右向上弯曲分开。有学者认为是鱼凫族族徽，属古巴蜀青铜兵器中罕有的珍品。

人虎纹戈
Dagger with figure and tiger pattern
战国（前475年～前221年）
通长24.6厘米
峨眉山博物馆藏

宽援，援侧有不对称长、短胡。长胡末端弯折成固定于柲的方牙，近阑处有三条形穿。援后部两面饰浅浮雕人虎纹，虎首在援末，怒目、竖耳、张口露齿，并形成齿形大穿。虎身在胡上，背阑腹刃，虎尾后曳，通体饰瓦形鳞片纹。虎口向锋，口下中脊上有一人，头结双髻，双手反缚跪地，头近虎口，应与文献中"以虎饮人血"的记载有关，为研究古代巴蜀文化提供了重要资料。

中胡戈
Medium minority dagger

战国（前475年～前221年）
通长20.8厘米
峨眉山博物馆藏
中胡三穿，援有凸脊直达锋端，长方形内上有水滴形穿。素面。

鸟纹长援戈
Long dagger with bird pattern

战国（前475年～前221年）
通长21厘米
峨眉山博物馆藏
长援起脊，援部两面均饰浅浮雕大眼鸟首，将脊巧妙地作为长尖喙。近本处有一圆穿、二条形穿。长方形内中部有一水滴形穿，近阑处有四条平行线，内上阴刻凹形双勾线纹饰。

虎纹中胡戈
Medium minority dagger with tiger pattern

战国（前475年～前221年）
通长 21.5厘米
峨眉山博物馆藏
宽援，中胡，胡末端弯折成牙，近阑处三条形穿。援后部两面饰浅浮雕虎纹，张口、卷尾，呈奔跑状。长方形内中有一圆穿。

龙纹中胡戈
Medium minority dagger with dragon pattern

战国（前475年～前221年）
通长19.4厘米
峨眉山博物馆藏
直援，中胡，胡末端有固定于柄的方牙，近阑处三穿。援后部两面饰浅浮雕龙纹、张口、长舌外吐、卷尾，呈腾云状。长方形内中一圆穿，近阑处有两条平行线。

Bronze Wares
049

凸穿十字形戈
Convex mounting cross-shape dagger

战国（前475年～前221年）
通长16.3厘米
峨眉山博物馆藏

长援有脊、短胡，与内呈十字形，近阑处有凸起心形大穿及二条形穿。长方形内上有橄榄形穿，近阑处有两条平行线。

十字形戈
Cross-shape dagger

战国（前475年～前221年）
通长24厘米
峨眉山博物馆藏

长援，有脊直达锋端，短胡，与内呈十字形，近阑处有一心形大穿、二条形穿。长方形内中部有一椭榄形穿，近阑处有四条平行线。

巴蜀文字戈
Dagger with Bashu characters

战国（前475年～前221年）
通长21厘米
峨眉山博物馆藏

直援，援腰微束，长胡上刻有铭文，近阑处有二长条形穿，援本处有一圆形穿。内呈长方形，饰几何形图案。该戈铭文为研究巴蜀文字提供了重要资料，实属古代巴蜀青铜兵器中罕有的珍品。

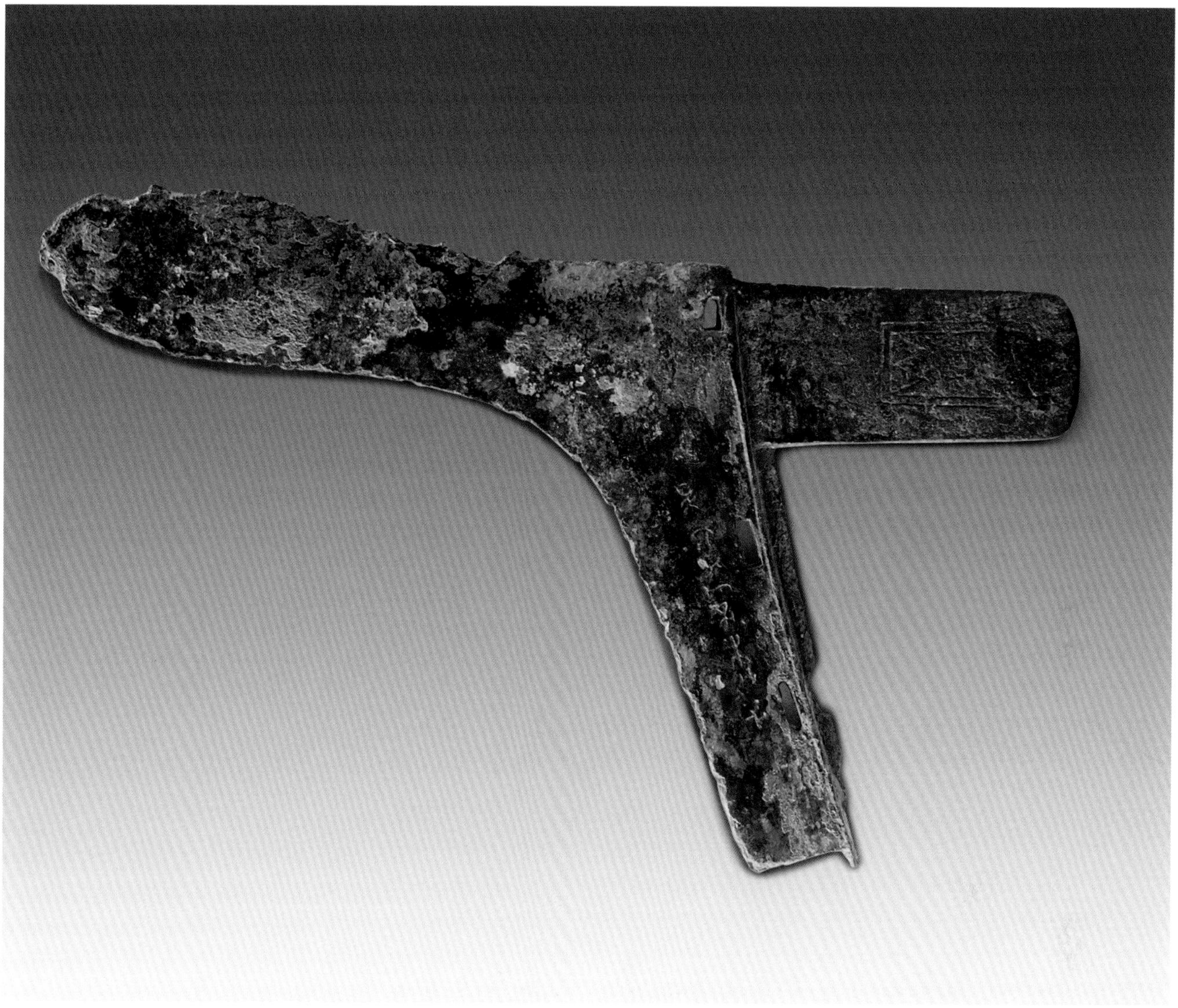

龙纹短骹宽叶矛
Broad spear with dragon patter

战国（前475年～前221年）
通高16.4厘米
峨眉山博物馆藏
短骹宽叶形、弓形双耳。骹部一面饰浅浮雕线条形龙纹；另一面阴刻虎形纹。

虎纹宽叶矛
Broad spear with tiger pattern

战国（前475年～前221年）
通高25.6厘米
峨眉山博物馆藏
短骹宽叶形、弓形双耳、圆銎直达矛端、骹身一面饰浅浮雕虎纹。

猎鹿纹宽叶矛
Broad spear with deer-hunting pattern

战国（前475年～前221年）
通高22.3厘米
峨眉山博物馆藏
短骹宽叶形、弓形双耳。骹身一面饰浅浮雕虎纹巴蜀图语；另一面饰猎鹿纹、一箭射出、鹿狂奔，应是战国时期蜀人狩猎生活的真实写照。

鱼凫纹宽叶矛
Broad spear with Yuhu pattern

战国（前475年～前221年）
通高36厘米
峨眉山博物馆藏
短骹宽叶形、弓形双耳。骹身饰鱼凫纹，骹端饰浅浮雕云雷纹一周。

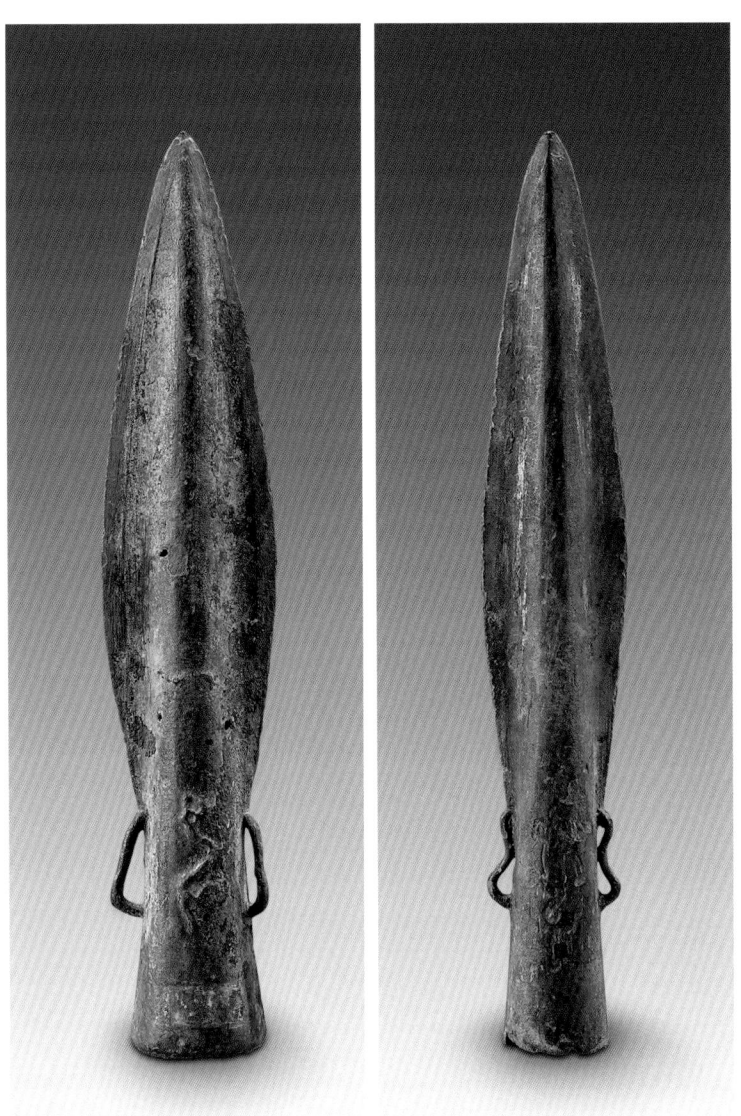

人虎纹宽叶矛
Broad spear with figure & tiger pattern

战国（前475年～前221年）
通高22.5厘米
峨眉山博物馆藏
短骸宽叶形、弓形双耳。骹身一面饰浅浮雕人虎纹，一虎张口拖尾，虎口向锋，口下有一双手反缚下跪之人；另一面饰手心纹组成的巴蜀图语。

长骸三穿双耳矛
Long-neck double-ear spear

战国（前475年～前221年）
通高22.2厘米
峨眉山博物馆藏
叶较宽，前锋锐而厚，刃两侧有血槽，圆銎直达矛尖，凸脊，长骸，三穿双耳、素面。

无耳中骸矛
Earless medium-neck spear

战国（前475年～前221年）
通高24.4厘米
峨眉山博物馆藏
骸较宽，前锋锐而厚，刃两侧有血槽，狭长条刃，近本部位稍扩成锐角形，凸脊直达矛尖。圆銎，上有图形符号，銎端略外弧。

楚式剑
Chu-style sword

战国（前475年～前221年）
通长50.7厘米
峨眉山博物馆藏
脊呈直线，斜宽从，狭前锷，实圆茎，茎上有二道凸箍，厚宽格，有首。

扁茎剑
Flat narrow sword

战国（前475年～前221年）
通长26.6厘米
峨眉山博物馆藏
腊下段较宽、上段收狭，脊呈凹形，身薄并铸虎皮纹，窄格，短扁茎。近格处一面阴刻虎纹；另一面刻手心纹。此剑与常见的战国巴蜀柳叶剑迥异，形制具有中原地区特色，从一个侧面反映了此时蜀地与中原地区有着密切的交流。

虎斑纹柳叶剑
Willow-leaf sword with dotted tiger pattern

战国（前475年～前221年）
通长39厘米
峨眉山博物馆藏
扁茎、无格、有二穿、身稍宽、柳叶状、鱼背脊直达锋端。身两面均饰虎斑纹，为典型的巴蜀式柳叶剑。

虎纹柳叶剑
Willow-leaf sword with tiger pattern

战国（前475年～前221年）
通长45.4厘米
峨眉山博物馆藏
扁茎、无格、有二穿、身稍宽、柳叶状、鱼背脊直达锋端。身基部两面均饰长身虎纹、口向锋，尾起卷处有巴蜀符号。

斧
Axe

战国（前475年～前221年）
通高18.3厘米
峨眉山博物馆藏
长方形銎，弧刃。近銎处有双勾折线纹。

斧
Axe

战国（前475年～前221年）
通高19.3厘米
峨眉山博物馆藏
矩形銎，弧刃较宽。銎部饰浅浮雕双勾折线纹。

鱼凫纹斤
Jin with Yuhu pattern

战国（前475年～前221年）
通高14.7厘米
峨眉山博物馆藏
长方形銎，直体，平刃。近銎处一面阴刻鱼凫纹；另一面饰双勾折线纹。

平肩圆刃钺
Flat shoulder round hole *yue*

战国（前475年～前221年）
通高19.3厘米
峨眉山博物馆藏
銎椭圆形，平肩，折腰，圆刃，骹有十棱。器身阴刻船形符号。

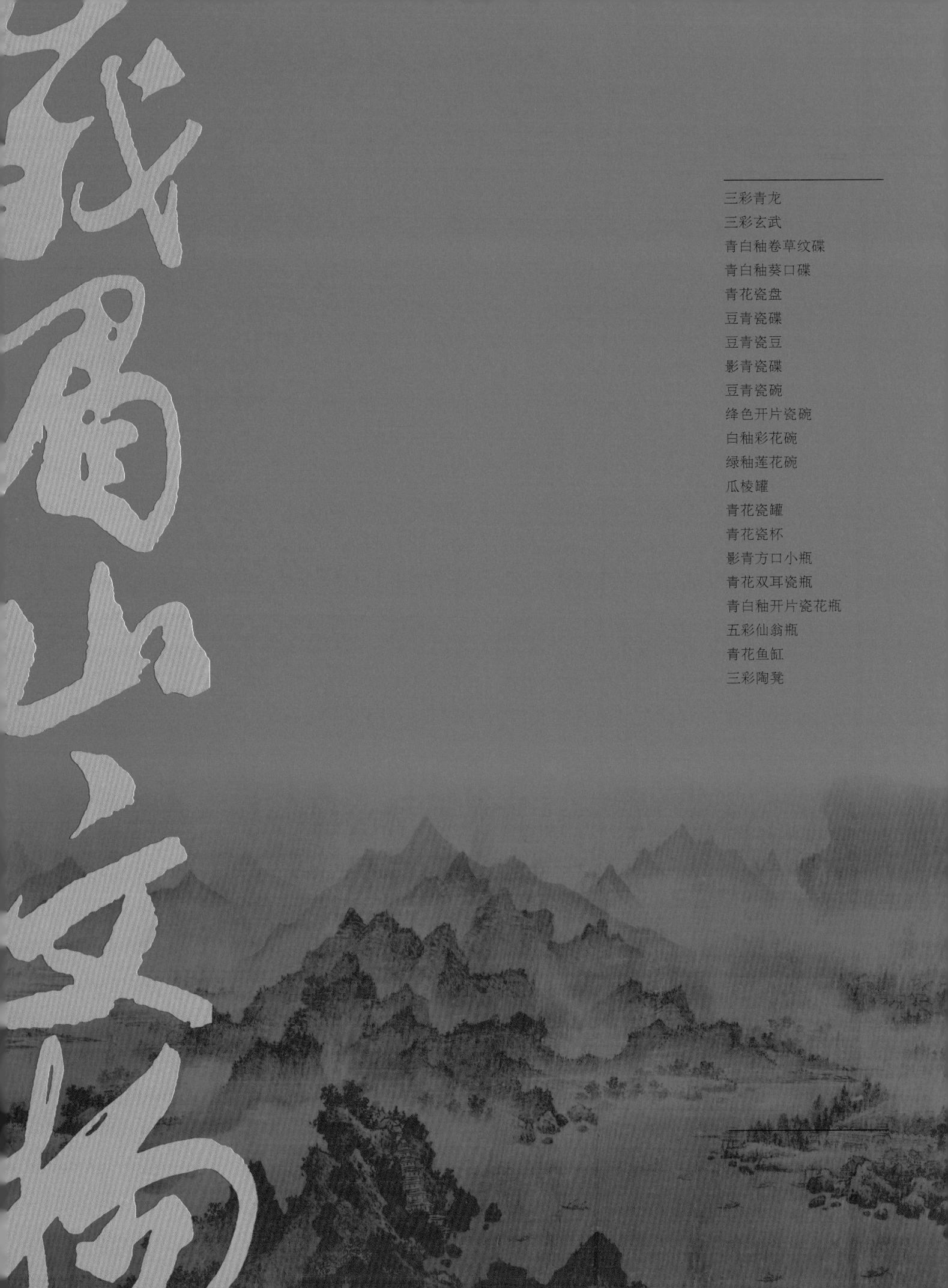

三彩青龙
三彩玄武
青白釉卷草纹碟
青白釉葵口碟
青花瓷盘
豆青瓷碟
豆青瓷豆
影青瓷碟
豆青瓷碗
绛色开片瓷碗
白釉彩花碗
绿釉莲花碗
瓜棱罐
青花瓷罐
青花瓷杯
影青方口小瓶
青花双耳瓷瓶
青白釉开片瓷花瓶
五彩仙翁瓶
青花鱼缸
三彩陶凳

峨眉山文物

陶瓷器
Porcelain Wares

062-089

三彩青龙
Three color blue dragon
宋（960~1279年）
通高14.9厘米
峨眉山博物馆藏
青龙亦称苍龙，在古代神话中代表东方，属四神之一。此青龙为双角、蛇形身、巨尾、四脚三爪、身饰鳞甲、昂首站立于长方形基座上。

三彩玄武
Three color Xuanwu
宋（960~1279年）
通高10.3厘米
峨眉山博物馆藏
玄武在古代神话中代表北方，为蛇缠龟，属四神之一。此玄武为一龟立于座上，背上一蛇。釉彩已大部脱落。

青白釉卷草纹碟
Blue & white porcelain dish of rolled-grass pattern

宋（960~1279年）
口径10.8厘米
峨眉山市文物管理所藏

敞口，圆唇，弧腹，腹壁有一明显凸棱，平底，底内凸。瓷胎洁白、细腻、坚硬。施天青釉，釉质莹润，釉色白中闪青。器底内壁饰内刻卷草纹。釉色纯正，纹饰精美，属景德镇湖田窑产品，在四川地区宋代窖藏中鲜见，十分珍贵。

青白釉葵口碟
Blue & white porcelain dish

宋（960~1279年）
口径10.8厘米
峨眉山市文物管理所藏

多瓣葵形缘，敞口、尖唇，弧腹，腹壁有二十四凸棱，平底，底微内凸。瓷胎洁白、细腻、坚硬。施天青釉，釉质莹润、釉色白中闪青，凹处集釉呈淡青色，凸处釉色泛白。釉色纯正，纹饰精美，属景德镇湖田窑产品，在四川地区宋代窖藏中鲜见，十分珍贵。

Porcelain Wares
067

青花瓷盘
Blue & white porcelain dish

明（1368～1644年）
通高3.5厘米
峨眉山博物馆藏
民窑作品。胎细、口沿外敞、圆腹。盘中绘一菠箩，其下有一"釉"字款。

豆青瓷碟
Bean green porcelain dish

南宋（1127～1279年）
通高3.3厘米
峨眉山博物馆藏
南宋墓葬出土。敞口、折沿外侈、斜壁、折下腹、平底、矮圈足。足部露胎处有铁锈红线一周。胎灰白，施豆青釉。

豆青瓷豆
Bean green porcelain bowl

南宋（1127～1279年）
通高9厘米
峨眉山博物馆藏
南宋墓葬出土。敞口、口沿外侈、斜弧腹、短柄中空，柄把有两道印痕，足微侈。口沿及足现铁锈红。灰白色胎，施豆青釉。

影青瓷碟
Shadowy blue porcelain plate

南宋（1127～1279年）
通高1.8厘米
峨眉山博物馆藏
南宋墓葬出土。敞口、斜壁、口沿和腹菊瓣形、平底。青白瓷，白胎质薄，芒口，银扣已脱落，内底印阴纹菏莲游鸭及回纹一周。

Porcelain Wares

071

豆青瓷碗
Bean green porcelain bowl
南宋（1127～1279年）
通高8.3厘米
峨眉山博物馆藏
敞口微侈、斜弧腹、圈足。胎灰白较厚，内外壁施满釉，外壁饰萱草花纹，圈足部施釉不全。

绛色开片瓷碗
Deep red porcelain bowl
明（1368～1644年）
通高10.3厘米
峨眉山博物馆藏
敞口、口折沿外侈、斜弧腹。内外施绛色釉，通体开冰裂纹。圈足、底沿无釉，露酱色胎。

Porcelain Wares

073

白釉彩花碗
White glazed color bowl

清（1644～1911年）
通高5.4厘米
峨眉山博物馆藏

敞口，口沿莲瓣形，深腹，圈足。白胎质薄，内外施白釉、釉色洁白晶莹、外壁绘有彩色缠枝花卉图案。

绿釉莲花碗
Green glazed lotus bowl
清—民国（1644～1949年）
通高6.1厘米
峨眉山博物馆藏
此碗形似一朵盛开的莲花。敞口微敛，口沿作莲瓣形，折腹平底。白胎质薄，内外施绿釉，釉色莹润。外壁饰浮雕粉红莲花，色泽鲜艳。

瓜棱罐
Melon-shape pot

宋（960～1279年）
通高8.4厘米
峨眉山博物馆藏
瓜棱形，直口，口沿残，短颈，鼓腹，平底。施灰白釉。

青花瓷罐
Blue & white porcelain pot

明（1368～1644年）
通高 57厘米
峨眉山博物馆藏
俗称"将军罐"。敛口、丰肩、平底。全器饰以婉转多姿的花卉缠枝。胎质均匀，属景德镇民窑的上品。

青花瓷杯
Blue & white porcelain mug
明（1368～1644年）
通高6.4厘米
峨眉山博物馆藏
景德镇民窑作品。直口、斜壁内收、底部有圈足。胎体轻薄，杯内外均绘青花缠枝花卉，底部和口沿内圈饰云雷纹。

影青方口小瓶
Shadowy blue square-mouth vase
南宋（1127～1279年）
通高16.1厘米
峨眉山博物馆藏
龙泉窑产品，胎灰白，施粉青釉。方形、口外撇，口沿与颈之间成折角，束颈，腹从上到下渐硕、矮方足。在露胎处有铁锈红线一周。

青花双耳瓷瓶
Blue double-handle vase

明（1368～1644年）
通高42厘米
峨眉山博物馆藏

直口、细颈、斜肩，其下逐渐侈张再内敛，圈足长而外侈。口沿下饰三角形几何纹一周，颈肩部绘有花卉，腹部是海星、螃蟹、虾，圈足部绘有奔驰的骏马。最引人入胜的是颈两侧的附耳，为两龙首口喷水注，形成双耳，可谓匠心独具。

青白釉开片瓷花瓶
Blue & white porcelain vase

清—民国（1644～1949年）
通高36.1厘米
峨眉山博物馆藏

仿哥窑作品。直口，口沿下饰云纹一周，短颈两端附一对兽耳、鼓腹、圈足。肩部饰云雷纹三道，足部饰云纹一周。青白色釉，器身满布褐色冰裂纹。

五彩仙翁瓶
Five-colour god vase

民国二年（1913年）
通高63厘米
峨眉山博物馆藏

釉上彩，直口，斜肩，底部稍内敛成圈足。瓶中央画的是数位仙翁欢聚的热闹场面，一位拄杖，一位抱伞，还有三位在观赏太极图。周围有假山花木和祥云瑞兽，并有数位憨态可鞠的仙童，或手捧仙桃，或手举葫芦，或手捧书卷。瓶颈画有两位仙童，或持灵芝，或捧仙果。这是近代民间比较喜欢表现的吉庆题材，画中充满了祥瑞气氛。

青花鱼缸
Blue & white porcelain fish tank

清（1644~1911年）
通高57厘米
峨眉山博物馆藏

直口，腹部以下逐渐内敛，平底。胎质均匀，釉色纯正、做工精美，其画工技法，在民窑作品里堪称一流。画中工笔勾勒出长廊、亭阁、花木，人物众多、衣冠楚楚、张灯结彩，其乐融融，应是当时大户人家奢华生活的写照。

三彩陶凳

Three-colour ceramic stool

清（1644～1911年）
通高52厘米
峨眉山博物馆藏

施红、绿、黄三彩。上部圆鼓形，肩四角饰兽首，其下逐渐内收，腹透空。属仿瓷鼓圆凳作品，其观赏价值超过了实用性能，在四川尚不多见。

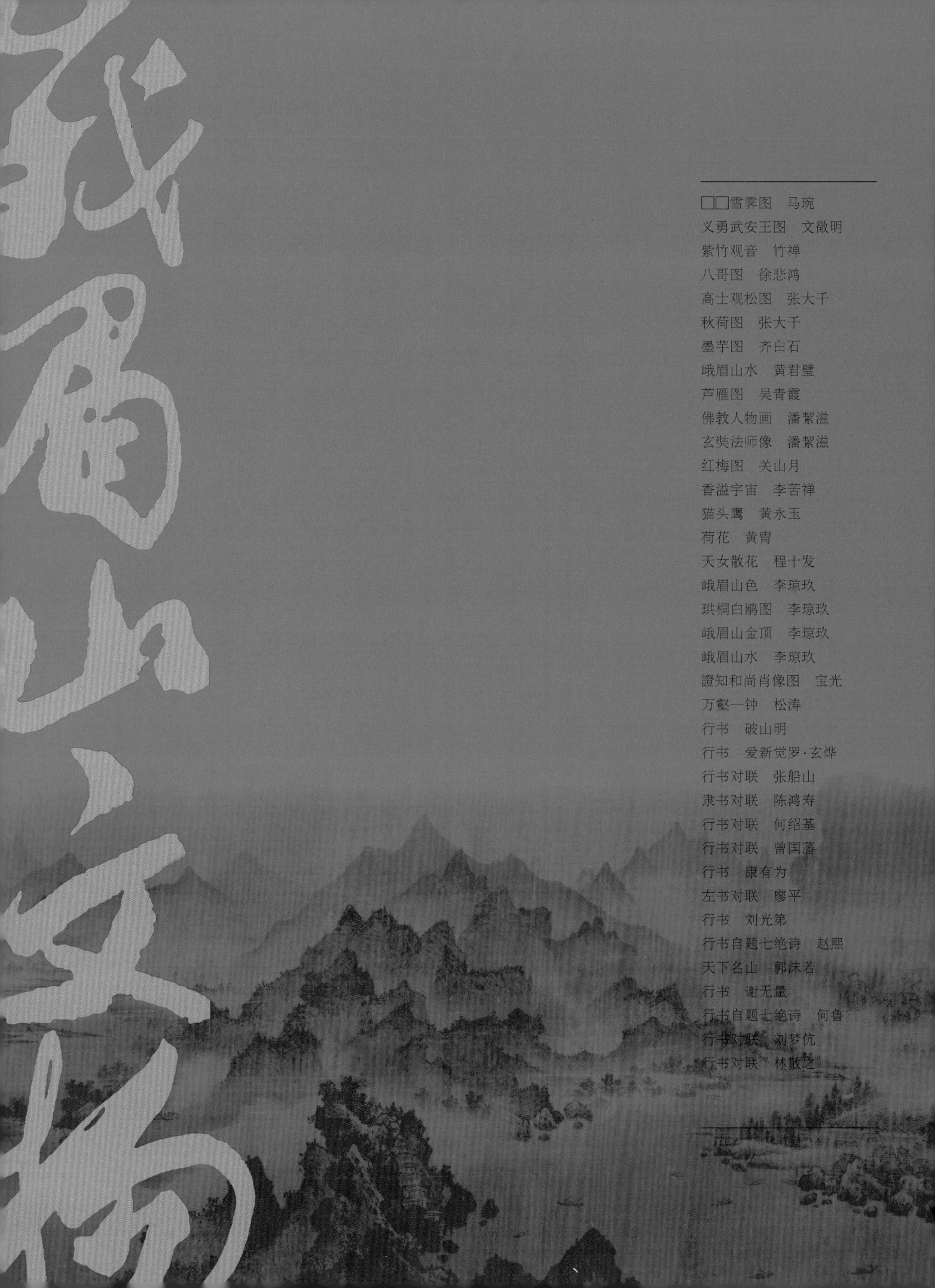

□□雪霁图　马琬
义勇武安王图　文徵明
紫竹观音　竹禅
八哥图　徐悲鸿
高士观松图　张大千
秋荷图　张大千
墨芋图　齐白石
峨眉山水　黄君璧
芦雁图　吴青霞
佛教人物画　潘絜滋
玄奘法师像　潘絜滋
红梅图　关山月
香溢宇宙　李苦禅
猫头鹰　黄永玉
荷花　黄胄
天女散花　程十发
峨眉山色　李琼玖
珙桐白鹇图　李琼玖
峨眉山金顶　李琼玖
峨眉山水　李琼玖
證知和尚肖像图　宝光
万壑一钟　松涛
行书　破山明
行书　爱新觉罗·玄烨
行书对联　张船山
隶书对联　陈鸿寿
行书对联　何绍基
行书对联　曾国藩
行书　康有为
左书对联　廖平
行书　刘光第
行书自题七绝诗　赵熙
天下名山　郭沫若
行书　谢无量
行书自题七绝诗　何鲁
行书对联　刘梦伉
行书对联　林散之

峨眉山文物

书画
Painting
and
Calligraphy Works of Famous Artists

090-135

□□雪霁图　马琬
Sunshine after Snow by Ma Wan

纸本
高197厘米　宽47.5厘米
峨眉山博物馆藏

上题隶书"□□雪霁图",下款行书"至正丁亥春作　文璧",钤白文"马文璧印"。其画层峦迭嶂、怪石嶙峋、微雪如霜。山中有古寺,重檐飞角。一流萦绕山间、虹桥横渡,上有一翁御驴而过,后随僮仆。

马琬,字文璧、号鲁钝生。金陵(今江苏南京市)人。元末明初画家,明洪武初官抚州(今江西抚州市)知府。

义勇武安王图 文徵明
Brave Wu'an Prince by Wen Zhenming

绢本
高205厘米 宽134厘米
峨眉山博物馆藏

工笔重彩绘义勇武安王（三国蜀将关羽封号）像。关羽中坐，戴冕旒，着王服，右侍关平捧金印，左侍周仓持偃月刀。画左落款"嘉靖五年夏四月浴佛日 奉佛弟子文壁盥手敬画"，钤白文印。全轴笔工严谨，线条苍润秀美，敷色艳丽而醇正。

文徵明（1470~1559年），初名壁，一作璧，以字行，更字徵明，号衡山居士。明代书画家，长州（今江苏吴县）人。与祝允明、唐寅、徐祯卿友善，人称"吴中四才子"。五十四岁任翰林院待诏。领"吴门画派"，与沈周、唐寅、仇英合称"明四家"。

净業釋子仔禪恭繪

紫竹观音 竹禅
Bamboo & Guanyin by Zhu Chan

纸本
高150厘米 宽81厘米
峨眉山佛教协会藏

竹禅，清代四川梁山（今梁平县）人，俗姓王，少年出家于梁山报国寺，受戒于双桂堂，通诗文，善书画，工篆刻。所绘竹虽只寥寥数笔，却姿态万千，形神兼备，清瘦中见俏丽，潇洒中见劲节，不娇不艳，不屈不挠，画出了竹的韵味。这幅"紫竹观音"中，观音端坐于竹林石上，画面清雅脱俗，展现了一种超凡的慈悲境界，应是竹禅书画中的精心之作。

八哥图 徐悲鸿
Birds by Xu Beihong

纸本
高111厘米 宽 31.5厘米
峨眉山博物馆藏

徐悲鸿既擅长传统国画，又长于油画，曾担任中央美术学院院长和中国美术家协会主席。其创作题材广泛，内容丰富，无论是山水、人物、奔马、鸟兽、花卉，无不落笔有神。这幅八哥图是徐悲鸿画给峨眉山果玲大和尚惠存的，并在题款中自述"所谓宋人意境而略变其趣"。画中八哥立于花枝，作顾盼状，生动而富有雅趣。

高士观松图 张大千
Pine Viewing by Zhang Daqian

纸本
高133厘米 宽65.3厘米
峨眉山博物馆藏

张大千，名爰，又名季爰，号大千、大千居士，画室名大风堂，四川内江人。他在绘画艺术方面博采众长，深谙各派技法而自成体貌，一生创作勤奋，享誉海内外。这幅高士观松图师古人画意，绘一位拄杖行走在松树下的高士，笔墨潇洒，意境隽永。

秋荷图 张大千
Autumn Lotus by Zang Daqian

纸本
高133厘米 宽68厘米
峨眉山博物馆。

张大千作为一代国画大师，在各种题材方面都造诣精深，而所绘荷花尤其绝妙。他喜欢采用泼墨写意的方式，来表现荷花的形态和神韵，深得其中三味，随意挥洒皆成佳作。这幅荷花图是张大千为一位居士所绘，笔墨之间也同样显示了一种随意的风格，却生动地显示了荷花亭亭玉立的韵味。

墨芋图　齐白石
Mo Yu Tu by Qi Baishi

纸本
高94.5厘米　宽33.5厘米
峨眉山博物馆藏

齐白石是近代中国最著名的书画大师，作品以写意为主，题材包罗万象，从人物、山水到花鸟、鱼虫、走兽，无所不精。笔墨奔放，挥洒自如。并精篆刻，工书法，善诗文，创作勤奋，画作甚多。这幅墨芋图是为果玲大和尚所画，寥寥几笔就极为传神地绘出了一幅亭亭玉立的墨芋，显示出一种幽雅的意境和淡远的禅机。

峨眉山水　黄君璧
Mt. Emei Scnery by Huang Junbi

纸本
高114厘米　宽46厘米
峨眉山博物馆藏

黄君璧、字君翁、广东南海人，著名画家。他擅长山水，尤以画云水瀑布而闻名于世，曾在世界各地多次举办画展。这幅峨眉山水图，是黄君璧早年和郎静山等人共游峨眉山时所绘，既有古人雅意，又有写生的妙趣，堪称佳作。

芦雁图　吴青霞
Swallow by Wu Qingxia

纸本
高97厘米　宽59.5厘米
峨眉山博物馆藏

现代著名女画家吴青霞，1910年出生于江苏常州武进县书画世家，初名吴德舒，号篆香阁主、龙城女史。自幼习画，12岁参加画展，上世纪30年代被誉为上海画坛奇女子。在画坛上曾以多面手著称，人物、花鸟、虫鱼、走兽、山水之类皆擅长，尤以画鲤鱼和芦雁最负盛名。90多岁依然耳聪目明，作画不止。吴老喜欢旅游，曾遍游名山大川。这幅芦雁图就是她1977年11月游峨眉山时所作，图中芦雁戏水，栩栩如生，远山如黛，江渚似镜，天际雁阵归来，墨彩浓淡相宜，充满诗情画意，可谓境界不凡，堪称经典之作。

佛教人物画 潘絜滋
Buddhist Figures by Pan Jiezi

纸本
四条幅 均高116.5厘米 宽66.5厘米
峨眉山博物馆藏

潘絜滋生于1915年，是和徐悲鸿、傅抱石、叶浅予、蒋兆和等同时代的老一辈著名画家。曾到敦煌临摹壁画，多次举办画展、先后在中国历史博物馆（今中国国家博物馆）、中国美术家协会、北京画院工作。专长于工笔重彩，尤其擅长历史题材和佛道人物。这四幅佛教人物画，取材于佛教故事，人物众多，形态生动，构图主次分明，布局疏密得当，融传统绘画和古代壁画技法于一体，应是作者此类绘画中的精心之作。

玄奘法师像　潘絜滋
Picture of Rabbi Xuanzang by Pan Jiezi

纸本
高107.5厘米　宽52.3厘米
峨眉山博物馆藏

著名画家潘絜滋，擅长历史题材和佛教人物画。这幅画便取材于唐代高僧玄奘的故事，对玄奘的形象作了精心的描绘。据题款可知其作画时间为1956年春天。图中玄奘身着百纳袈裟，手持经卷，神态儒雅，可谓是此类画中的传神之作。

红梅图　关山月
Red Plum by Guan Shanyue

纸本
高96.5厘米　宽59厘米
峨眉山博物馆藏

关山月，原名泽霈，广东阳江人，早年曾游历各地和写生，多次举办画展，是当代"岭南画派"的代表画家。1959年与傅抱石合作为北京人民大会堂正厅创作大型国画"江山如此多娇"，1979年又为北京人民大会堂东厅创作大幅国画"春天南粤"。这幅红梅图，是关山月1981年春游峨眉山时，在报国寺中所绘。虽然他自谦为"急就"而成，仍挥洒自如，出手不凡，画出了翠竹的勃勃生机和老梅迎春绽放。

香溢宇宙 李苦禅
Fragrance Allover by Li Kuchan

纸本
高83厘米 宽50厘米
峨眉山博物馆藏

画心写春兰，并以山石、百哥点缀期间。兰以水墨润笔出叶，以嫩绿点卉。气势阔健，生机勃勃，馨香沁人。上端横书"香溢宇宙"四字，后跋"戊午岁末八十一叟苦禅写于京华"，钤白文"李"，朱文"苦禅"印。引首钤朱文"神州艺父"。

李苦禅（1898~1983年），山东高唐人。现代画家、美术教育家，中央美术学院教授。其大写意花鸟颇有特色，笔墨雄阔，气势磅礴。

猫头鹰 黄永玉
Owl by Huang Yongyu

纸本
高94厘米 宽69厘米
峨眉山博物馆藏

出生于湖南凤凰的土家族人黄永玉，作为中央美术学院教授和中国美术家协会副主席，在创作上喜作彩墨，不拘成法，擅长山水、花鸟、人物，其取材布局常别出心裁，给人以意境高古隽永之感，并擅长于版画与木刻插图，享有盛誉。据题款可知，此画是十年动乱后，乐山籍画家李琼久先生为峨眉山文管所求得此画。虽然此画用笔不多，却挥洒自如，猫头鹰的两只眼睛一睁一闭，更显得妙趣横生。

荷花 黄胄
Lotus by Huang Zhou

纸本
高69厘米 宽67.5厘米
峨眉山博物馆藏

黄胄，原名梁黄胄，河北蠡县人，长期从事绘画专业创作，擅长画人物、动物，尤其善画毛驴、骆驼等。这幅荷花图绘于峨眉山下，有题诗"峨眉新雨后，仙女夜弹琴"。画中荷花绽放，荷叶上有青蛙一对，作雨后欢鸣状。并将雨后在峨眉山下欣赏蛙鸣，比喻为仙女弹琴，是一种多么快乐和幽默的心情啊！

天女散花 程十发
Fairy Maiden & Flowers by Cheng Shifa

纸本
高135.5厘米 宽67.5厘米
峨眉山博物馆藏

程十发，原名潼，上海松江人，斋室取名步鲸楼、不教一日闲过之斋、三釜书屋。擅画人物、山水、花鸟，并长于连环画、年画、插图等。这幅天女散花图，为程十发在峨眉山报国寺所绘，画中的仙女显得端庄祥和，与通常的宗教绘画不同，虽然身着古装，但有着浓厚的现代写生气息，可谓别出心裁之作。

峨眉山色　李琼玖
Emei Mountain by Li Qiongjiu

纸本
高151厘米　宽176厘米
峨眉山博物馆藏

李琼久，乐山五通桥人，笔名九翁、九公、九躬、会宗堂居士、离垢园客人，斋名"永好堂"，曾与石鲁为同学，历尽磨难，创办嘉州画院。他的画作，意境深远，气势宏大，被称誉为布衣书画大师。这幅"峨眉山色"中堂，用浓墨画出苍劲的松树，以彩笔绘描远景山色，层次分明，错落有致，于沉静中绽放热情，在含蓄中彰显大气，显得极富诗意，可谓出手不凡，属画中佳品。

珙桐白鹇图　李琼久
Gong Tong Bai Xian Tu by Li Qiongjiu

纸本
高182厘米　宽99厘米
峨眉山博物馆藏

属水墨淡彩小写意。上题峨眉山文管所补白，落款"九躬琼久"，钤"九公书画"朱文印。白鹇与珙桐树均是峨眉山具有代表性的动植物，被尊称为"李峨眉"的李琼久先生以彩墨写实的手法将二者有机地结合起来，使白鹇栩栩如生，活脱脱呈现在观众面前，呼之欲出。

峨眉山金顶 李琼玖
Jinding of Mt. Emei by Li Qiongjiu

纸本
高96厘米 宽59厘米
峨眉山博物馆藏
这是一幅构思奇特的大气之作，被晨曦染红的峭壁山岩占据了整幅画面，山脚下一人在仰望山巅金顶，以此衬托了峨眉山的巍峨，显示出气势磅礴的景象。

峨眉山水 李琼玖
Mt. Emei Scenery by Li Qiongjiu

纸本
高68厘米 宽59厘米
峨眉山博物馆藏
作者采用写实的笔法，描绘了峨眉山中苍劲的松林、鲜艳的树木，在浅黛色的远山衬托下，显得生机勃勃而又意境隽永。

Painting and Calligraphy Works of Famous Artists

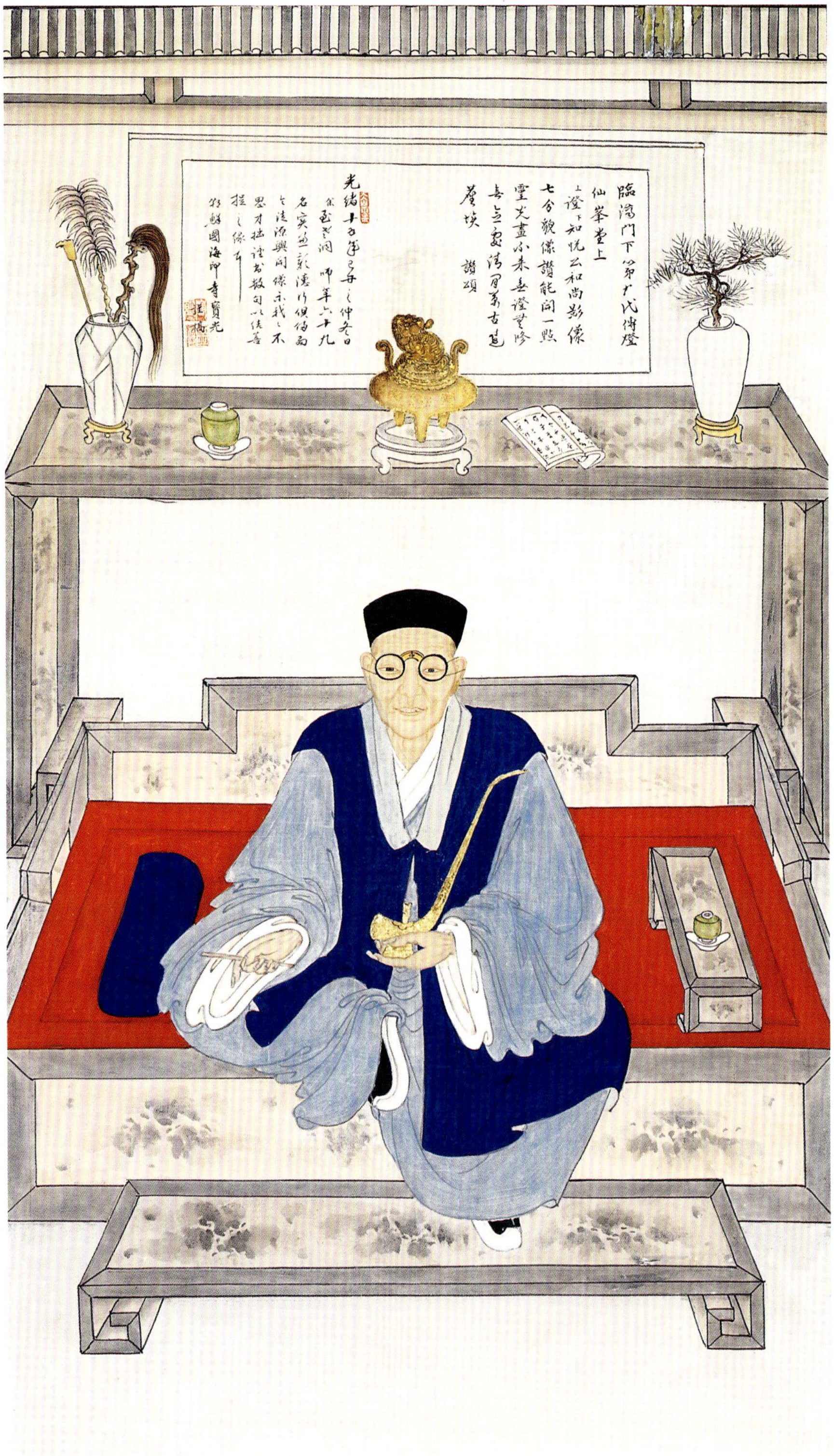

證知和尚肖像图
宝光（朝鲜）
Monk Zhengzhi by Bao Guang

纸本
高110厘米 宽62厘米
峨眉山佛教协会藏
清光绪十五年（1889年）作品，描绘了年事已高的證知和尚坐在僧榻上，戴着眼镜手持烟斗的情景，后面几案上有打开的书卷。较为真实地反映了当时僧侣的生活情形。

万壑一钟
松涛（日本）
Wan Hu Yi Zhong by Song Tao

纸本
高170厘米 宽87厘米
峨眉山佛教协会藏
清宣统三年（1911年）日本沙门松涛游览峨眉山九老洞画，赠海良和尚。图中绝壁万仞，苍松挺拔，葱郁的林木山色中露出寺庙一角，于幽远的意境中仿佛传来古刹钟声。

行书 破山明
Running script by Po Shanming

纸本
高112厘米 宽32厘米
峨眉山博物馆藏

破山明是明清之际的一位高僧，俗姓蹇，名海明，号旭东，四川大竹县人。出家为僧后，曾赴浙江宁波天童寺拜密云为师，受其嫡传，后回川，住梁平县太平寺。他精通释典，能诗善画，与四川当时的高官、文人学士关系友善，常有往来。圆寂后葬梁平双桂堂，著有《破山禅师语录》二十一卷。这幅书法为破山明用行草书写的两句诗，寓禅机于平淡之中，是其惯有的风格。

行书 爱新觉罗·玄烨
Running script by Xuan Ye

绢本
高107.7厘米 宽38.7厘米
峨眉山博物馆藏

清康熙皇帝统治时期，曾励精图治，促使了国家的兴旺，并重视民族团结，对宗教也比较宽容。这幅赐给峨眉山元享和尚的书法，便表达了康熙对忠厚朴诚的赞赏，以及对名山古刹的关注。

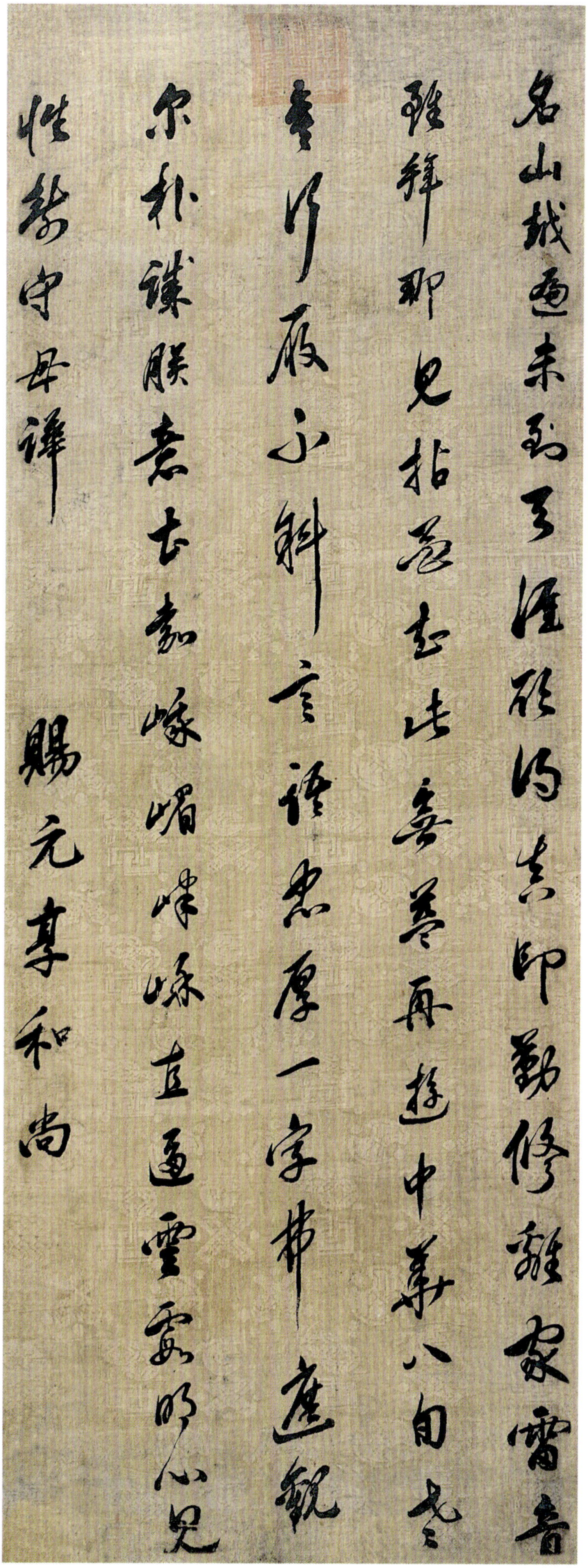

名山跋涉未為了匪惟朕勤修雖家鄉
雖拜聊見拈花去住无牽掛再掭小自登
峯巾履小科言語忠厚一字亦逾銳
尓朴謙朕喜去嘉峩峭崒直遶雲霄明心見
性勞勞守母諼
賜元孝和尚

行书对联 张船山
Couplet in running script by Zhang Chuanshan

纸本
高131.5厘米 宽34厘米
峨眉山博物馆藏

行书"诗称孟六文欧九，家在湖东屋瀼西"。落款"船山 张问陶"。钤白文"张问陶印"，另有朱白各半"船山"印一方。

张船山（1746～1814年），名问陶、字仲冶、号船山，亦号蜀冠仙史，四川遂宁人。清代诗人，书画家。乾隆五十五年（1790年）进士，任山东莱州府（今掖县）知府。

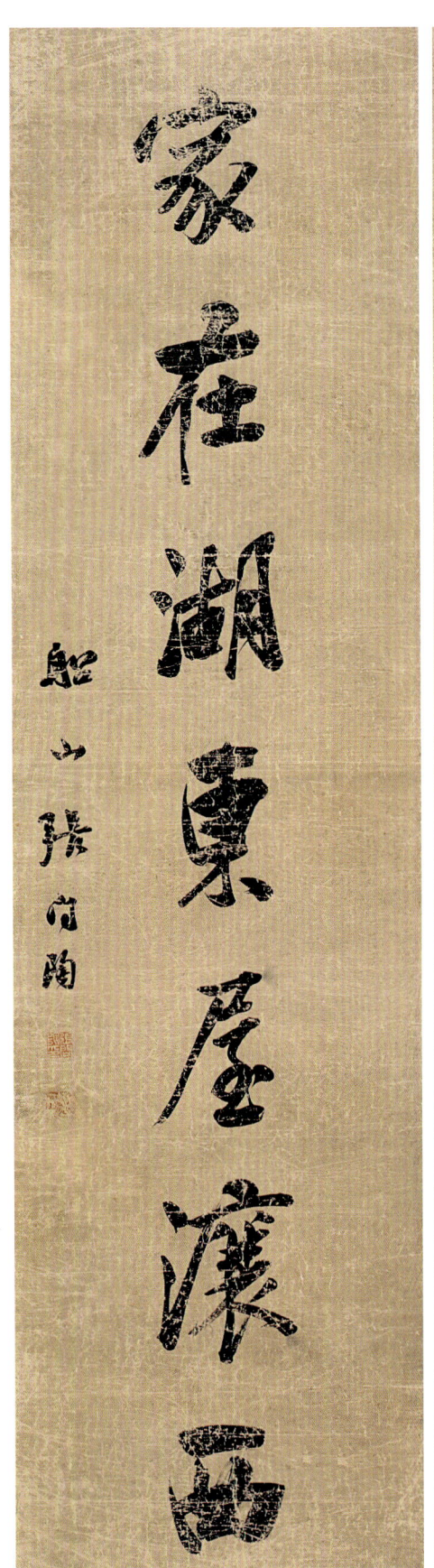
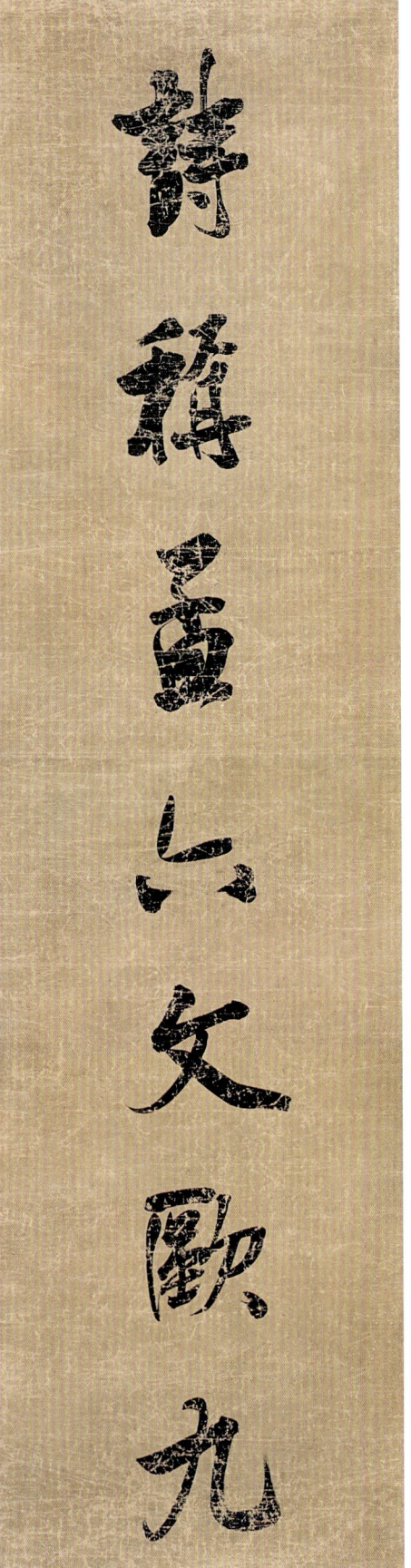

隶书对联　陈鸿寿
Couplet in Lishu Script by Chen Hongshou

纸本
高160.5厘米　宽39.5厘米
峨眉山博物馆藏

隶书"敬彼灵祇降其福庆，服君肃雅臻兹高年"。上题"集桐柏淮源庙碑"，落款"陈鸿寿"，钤白文"陈鸿寿印"、朱文"曼生"。隶近八分书，古拙富金石味。

陈鸿寿（1768～1822年），字子恭，号曼生，又号曼寿、曼公，别号种榆道人、夹谷亭长。浙江钱塘（今杭州）人，清代篆刻家、书法家、制陶家。嘉庆六年（1801年）拔贡，官淮安同知。篆刻取法秦汉，擅切刀，纵势爽利，为西泠八家之一。与陈豫钟齐名，世称"二陈"。著有《种榆仙馆印谱》、《桑连理馆集》等书。

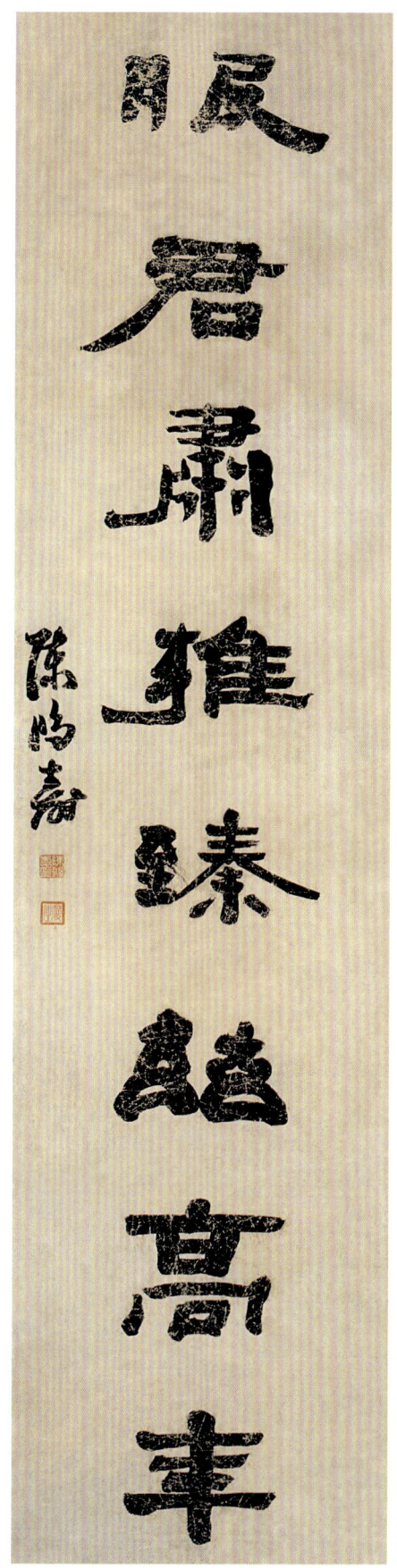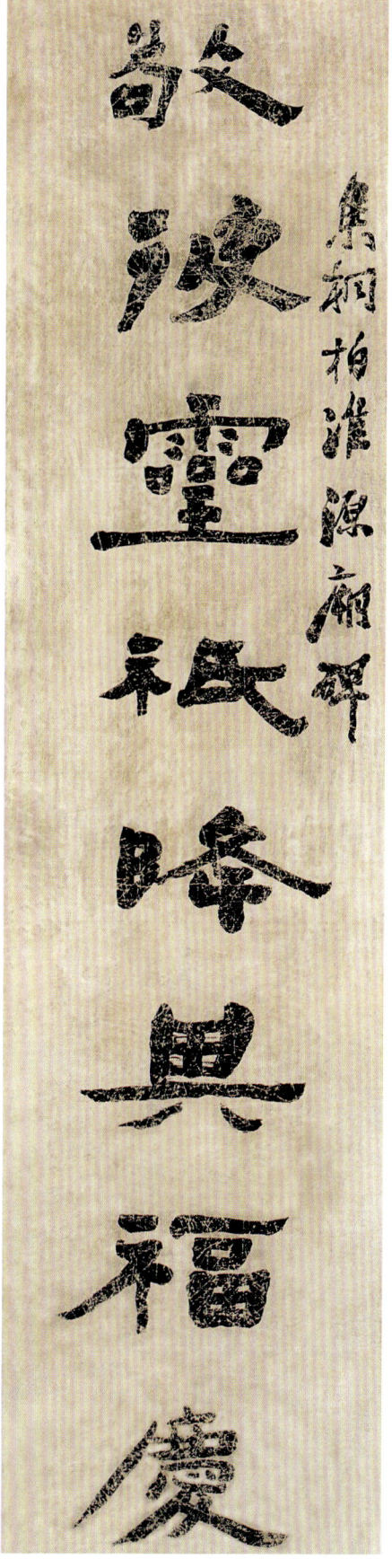

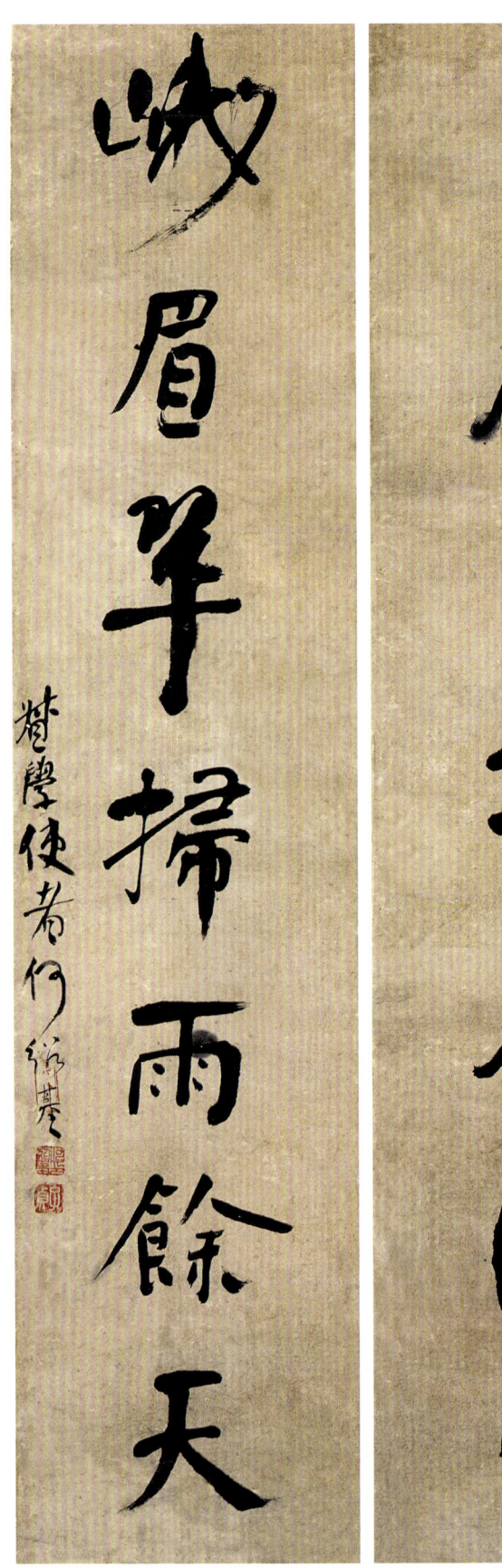
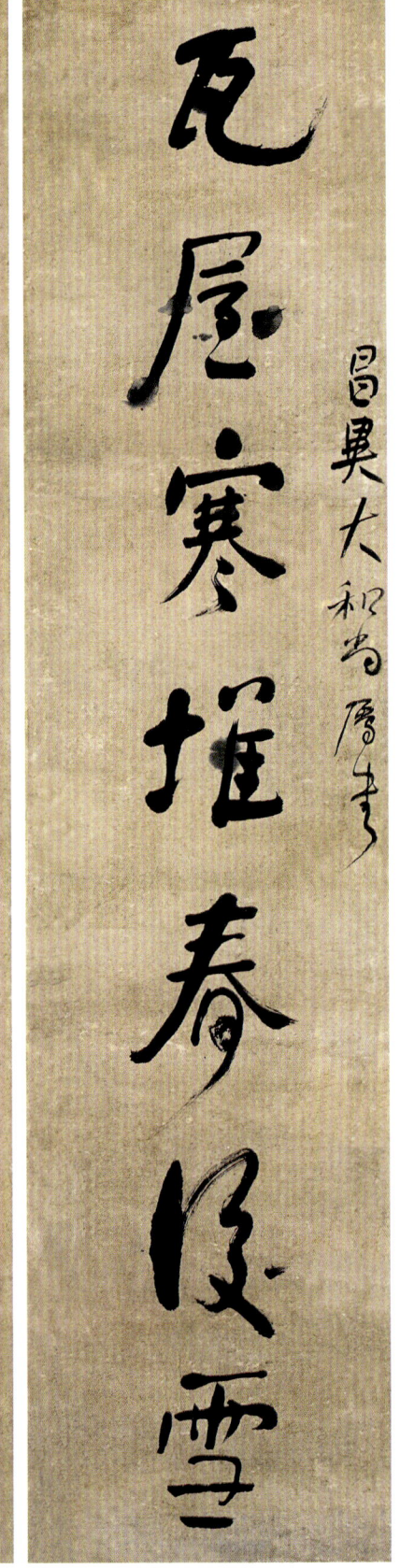

行书对联 何绍基
Couplet in running script by He Shaoji

纸本
高136.5厘米 宽31厘米
峨眉山博物馆藏

行书"瓦屋寒堆春后雪，峨眉翠扫雨余天"。上题"昌昇大和尚属书"，落款"督学使者何绍基"。款下朱白文"何绍基印"、白文"子贞"，款中有一长方印，印文不清。此联书近颜真卿，参有北魏碑意，实为书门别调。

何绍基（1799~1873年），字子贞，号东州居士，晚号猿叟，湖南道州（今道县）人。清代诗人、书法家。道光十六年（1836年）进士，官翰林院编修，咸丰壬子（1852年）为四川学政。通经史、小学，诗崇苏轼、黄庭坚。书宗颜真卿，取北魏碑版意趣，另成一体。

行书对联　曾国藩
Couplet in running script by Zeng Guofan

纸本
高171.1厘米　宽30.5厘米
峨眉山博物馆藏

行书"石床润极琴丝静，玉座尘消砚水清"。上题"净土禅院大和尚补壁法政"，落款"涤生曾国藩"。款下钤白文"曾国藩印"，朱文"涤生"。其书结体严谨，运笔不苟。

曾国藩（1811～1872年），字涤生、号伯涵，湖南湘乡人，原名子城。清道光十八年（1838年）进士、湘军统帅，有《曾文正公全集》。

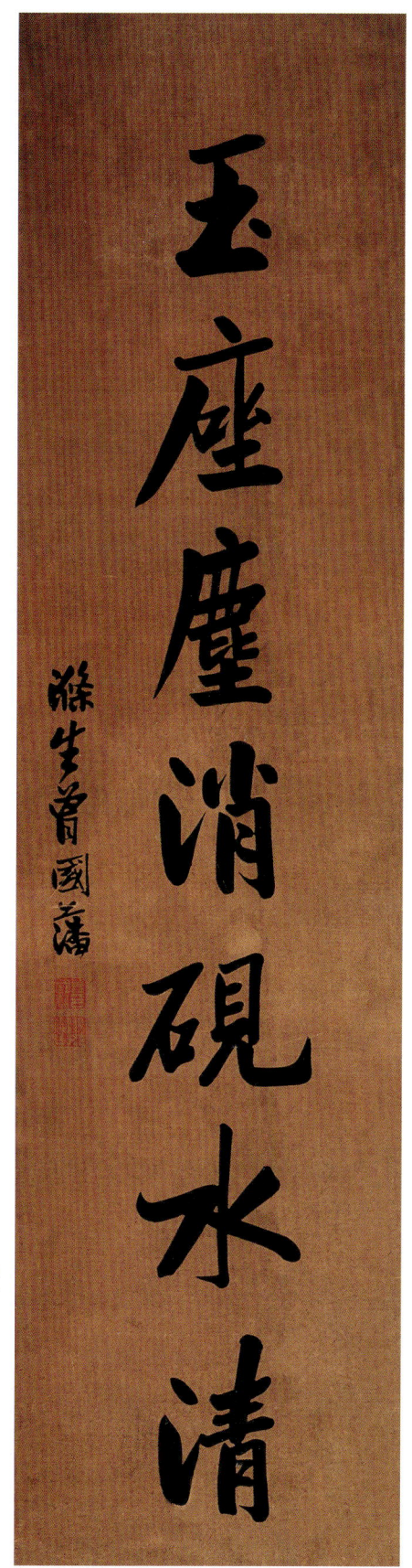
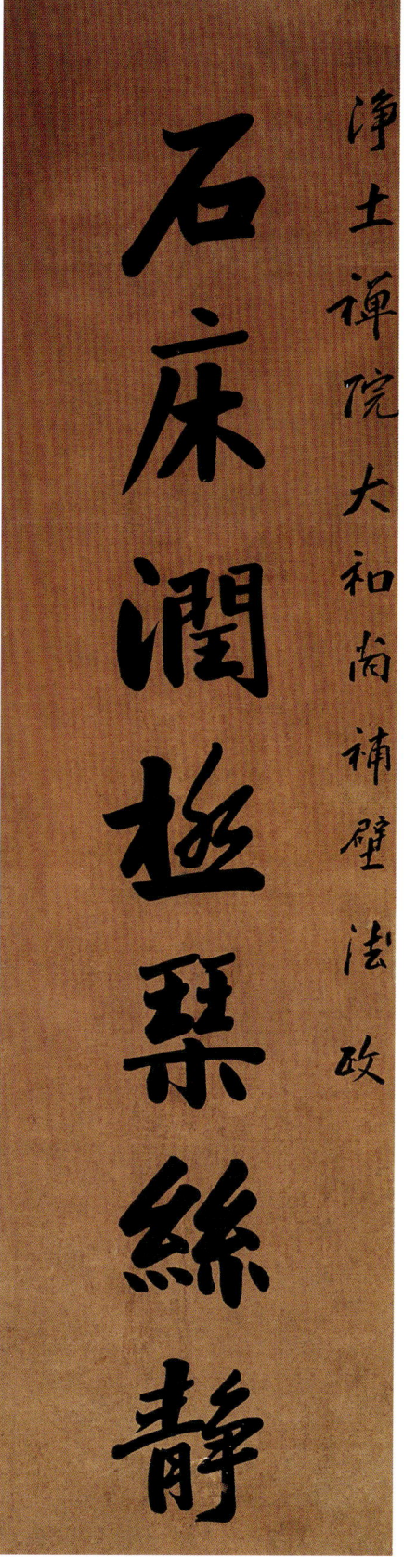

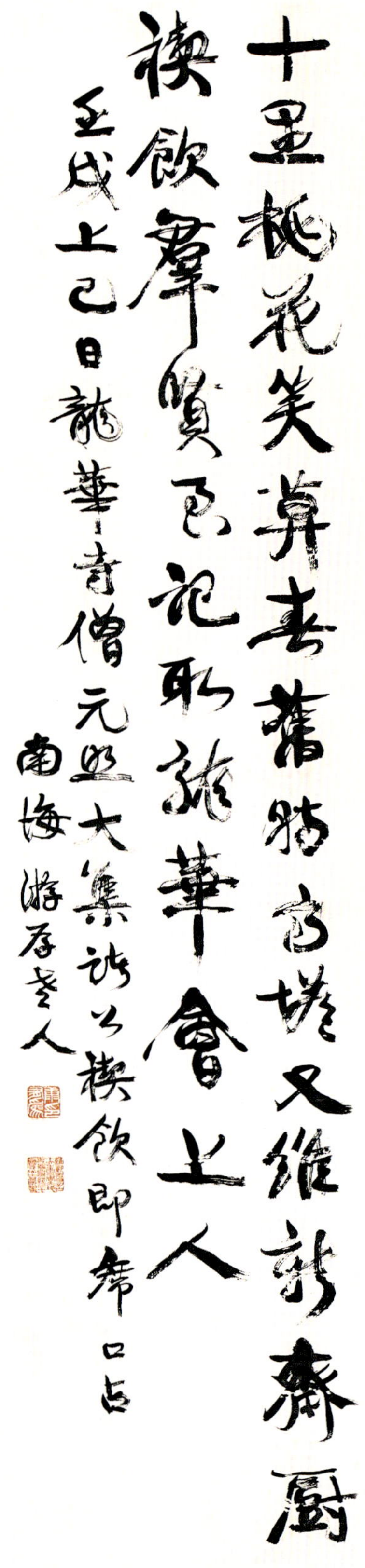

行书　康有为
Running script by Kang Youwei

纸本
高158.5厘米　宽35厘米
峨眉山博物馆藏

行书自题七言诗"十里桃花笑暮春，旧时高塔又维新。斋厨禊饮群贤至，记取龙华会上人"。落款"壬戌上巳日龙华寺僧元照大集诸公禊饮即席口占。南海游为老人"。其书运腕独特、用笔求拙、富魏碑意趣。此轴1922年书于上海龙华寺，后由该寺僧元照携来峨眉山。

康有为（1858～1927年），原名祖诒，字广厦、号长素、更生，晚年别号游为，广东南海人。清光绪进士。清"百日维新"的领导者。

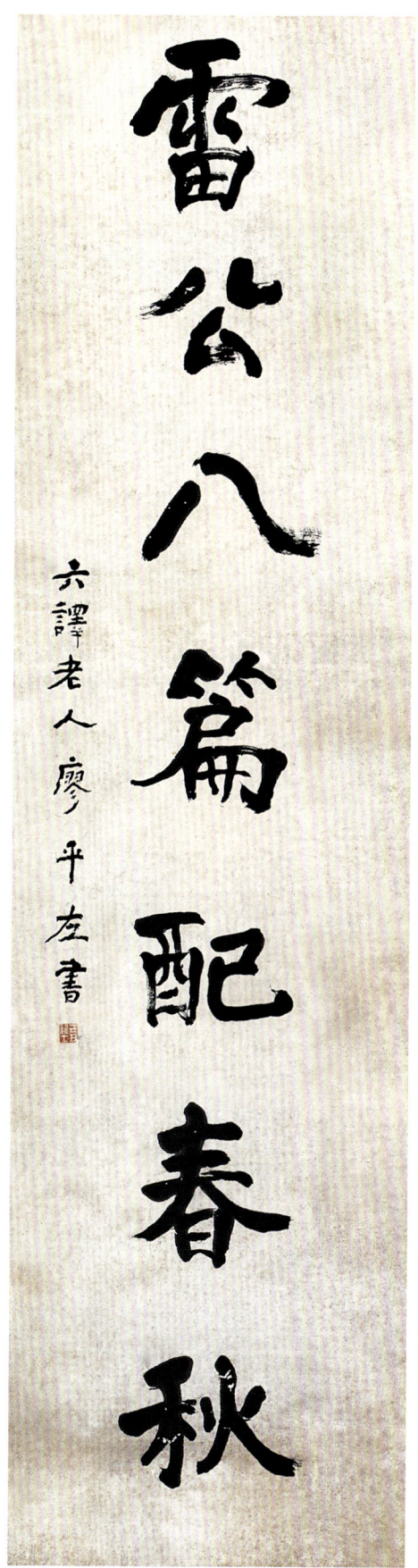

左书对联 廖平
Couplet of left-script by Liao Ping

纸本
高174.9厘米 宽45.5厘米
峨眉山博物馆藏

楷书"黄帝六相说诗易，雷公八篇配春秋"。上题"星桥先生正属"，落款"六译老人廖平左书"。钤白文"己丑进士"印。其书谋篇平正，结体精密古拙。因系左书，当为1920年后之作。

廖平（1852~1932年），原名登廷，字旭陔；后改名平、字季平，四川井研人。清光绪进士，民国后任四川（亦称成都）国学院院长多年。

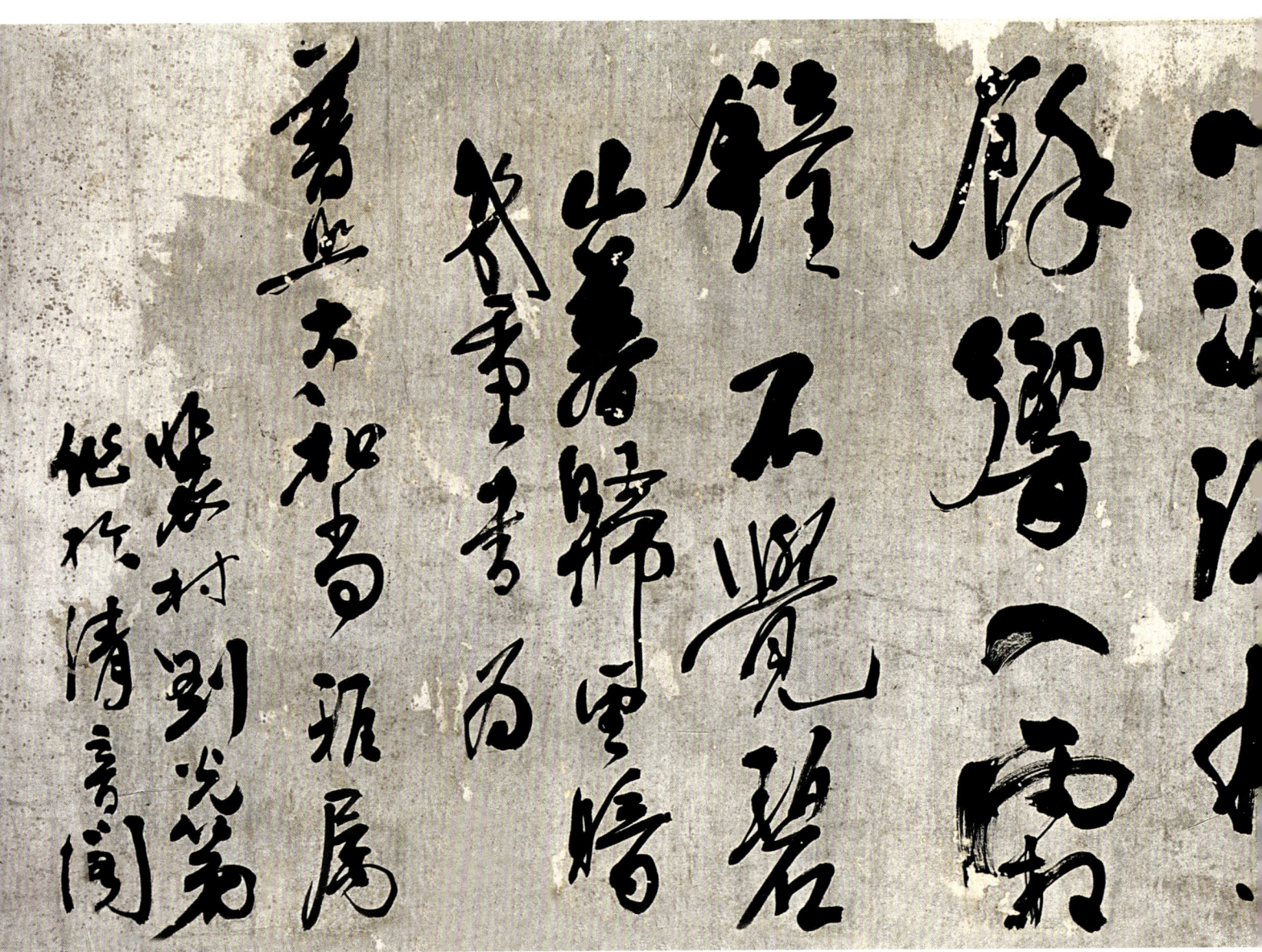

行书 刘光第
Running script by Liu Guangdi

纸本
高51厘米 宽144厘米
峨眉山博物馆藏

行书唐人李白《听蜀僧浚弹琴》诗。落款"普照大和尚雅属 裴村 刘光第作于清音阁"。
刘光第（1859~1898年），字裴村，四川富顺县人。光绪九年（1883年）进士。为"戊戌六君子"之一，著有《衷圣斋文集》、《介白堂诗集》、《游峨眉诗六十三首》。

蜀僧抱綠綺西下峨眉峰為我一揮手如聽萬壑松

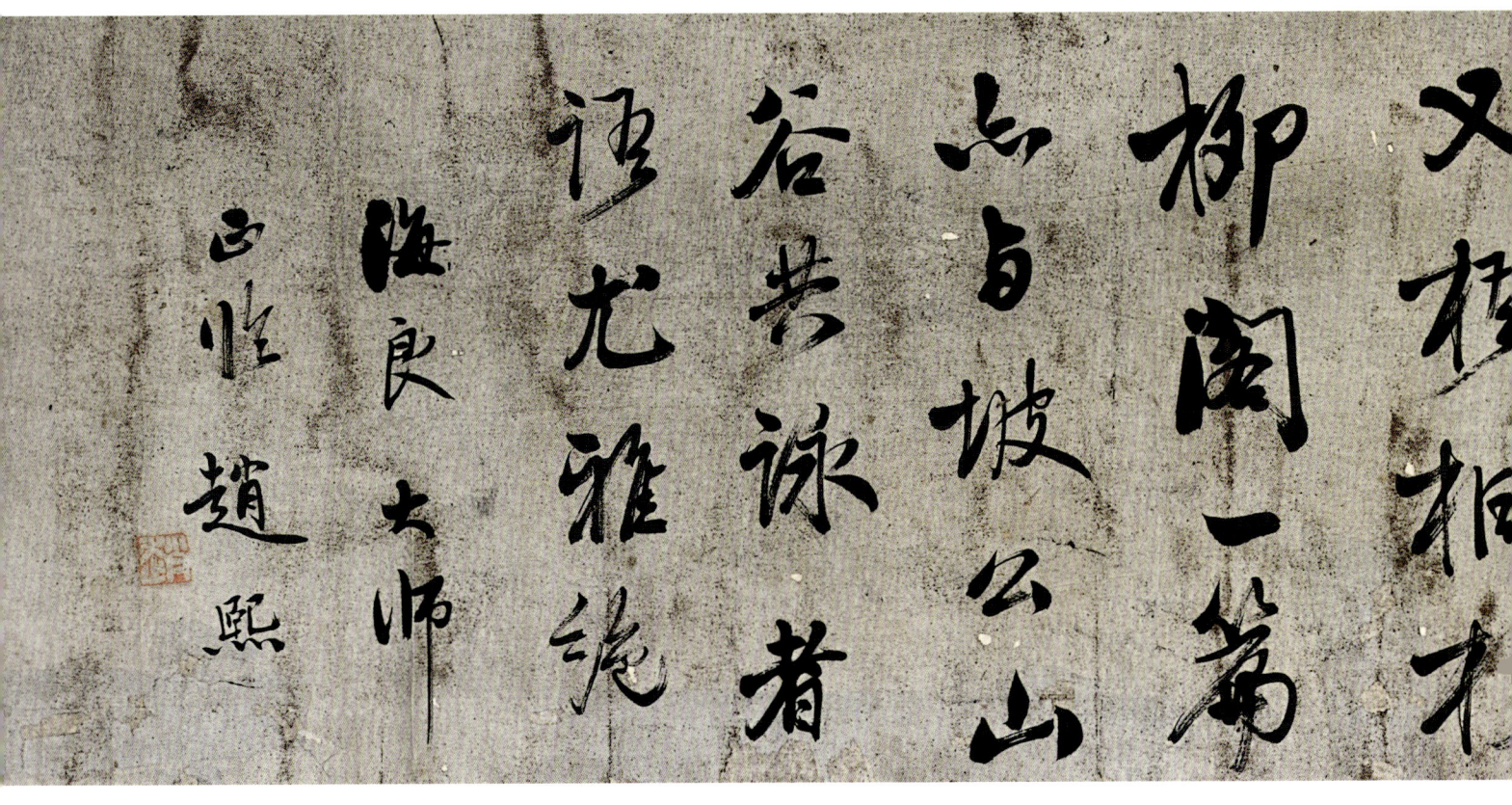

行书自题七绝诗　赵熙
Four-line Poem in Running Script by Zhao Xi

纸本
高33厘米　宽137厘米
峨眉山博物馆藏

行书自题七绝诗："淡墨秋山画远天，暮霞还照紫添烟；故人好在重携手，不到平山漫五年"。后题："又梧桐杉柳阁一篇，亦与坡公山谷共，咏者语尤雅绝。海良大师正雅"落款"赵熙"，款下钤白文"赵熙"印。其书稳健秀逸、笔墨高古，行而不放，颇见功力。
赵熙（1867～1948年），字尧生，号香宋，自题雪王龛，四川荣县人。清末民初学者、诗人、书画家。清光绪十七年（1891年）进士。

淡墨秋山畫遠天 暮霞還照紫添烟 故人好在重攜手 不到平山謾五年

天下名山　郭沫若
Famous Mountain under Heaven by Guo Moruo

纸本
高26.4厘米　宽84.4厘米
峨眉山博物馆藏

峨眉乃天下名山，郭沫若为近现代乐山名人，是遐迩闻名的大书法家，由他题写的这件横幅，刚柔有力，潇洒奔放，可谓书法作品中的精品。这幅题字已刻于峨眉山入口牌坊上，与青山绿树相辉映。

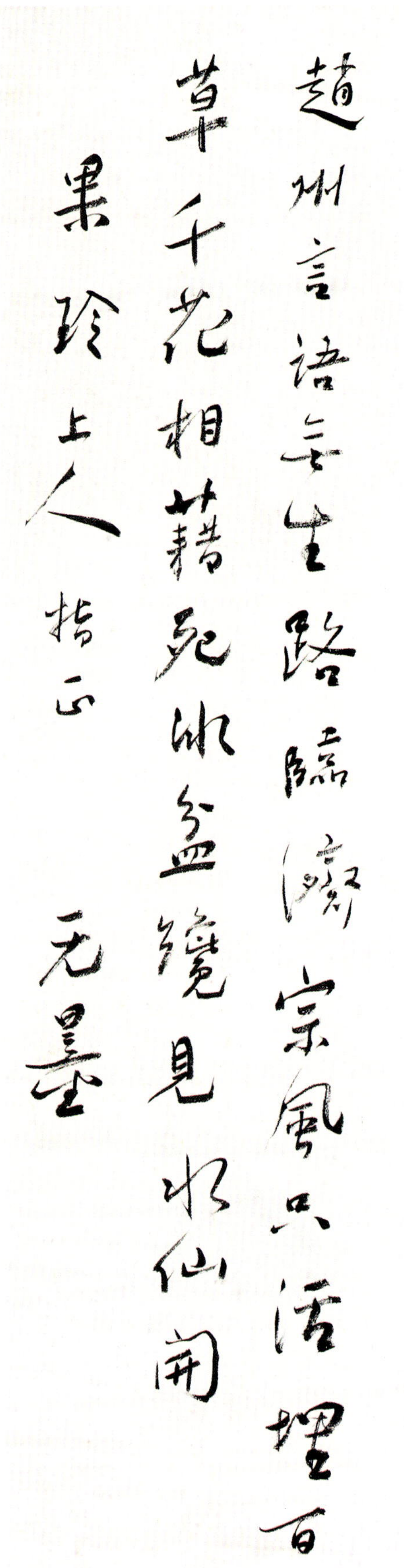

行书　谢无量
Running script by Xie Wuliang

纸本
高113厘米　宽29.7厘米
峨眉山博物馆藏

行书自题七绝诗一首"赵州言语无生路，临济宗风只活埋。百草千花相藉死，冰盆才见水仙开"。上题"果玲上人指正"，落款"无量"。其书法二王，虽变化多端，而精蕴不渝；吸取北碑的凝重散朗，天趣横生，自创一格。按其行止，应为1946年夏秋之际所作。

谢无量（1884~1964年），名大澄，字仲清，号希范，别号庵，四川乐至县人。先后任教于广州大学、东南大学、人民大学、四川大学。其书法独具一格，俗称"孩儿体"。

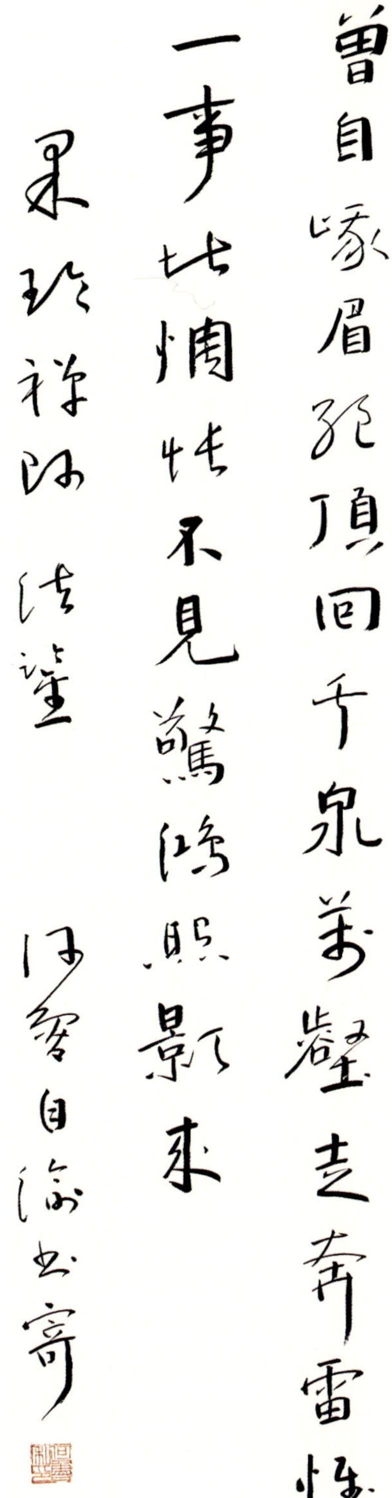

行书自题七绝诗　何鲁
Four-line Poem in Running Script by He Lu

纸本
高126.2厘米　宽31.7厘米
峨眉山博物馆藏

自题七绝诗"曾自峨眉绝顶回，千泉万壑走奔雷。惟余一事此惆怅，不见惊鸿照影来"。上题"果玲禅师法鉴"，落款"何鲁自渝书寄"，款下钤朱文"何鲁制印"印迹。

何鲁（1894～1973年），字奎恒，四川广安县人。现代数学家、书法家、教育家。其书法颜柳，兼欧苏，溶二王笔意，饶汉碑遗味，自成一格。曾任东南大学、中山大学、重庆大学教授达四十年之久。

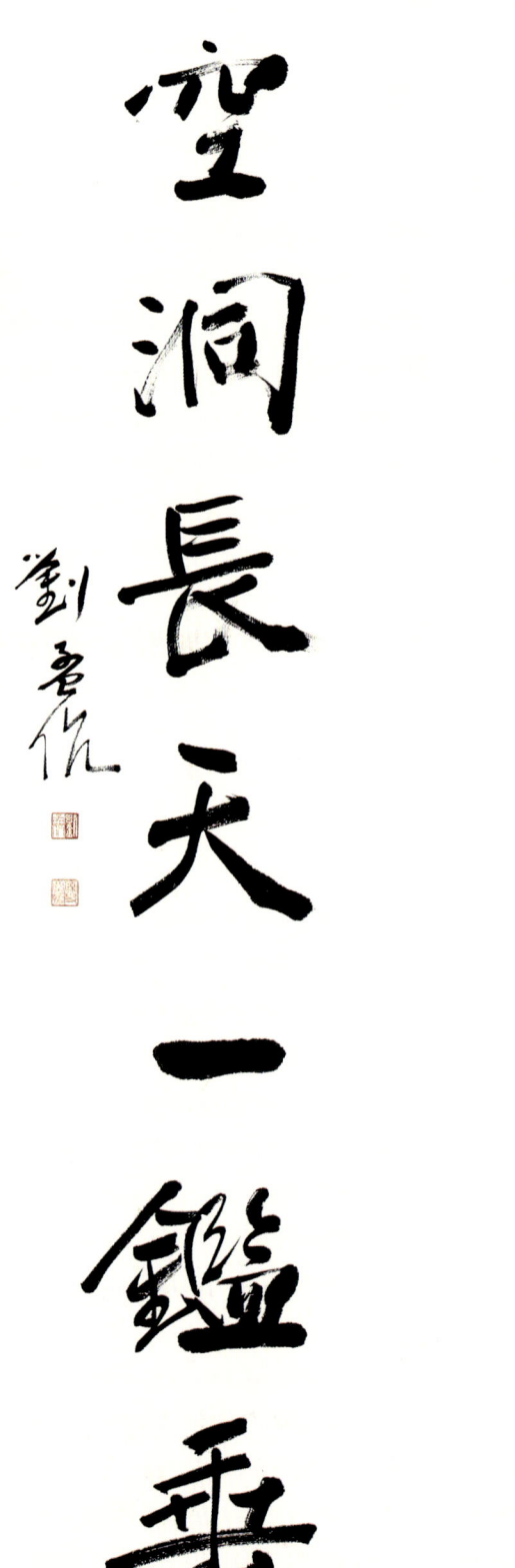

行书对联 刘梦伉
Couplet in running script by Liu Menghang

纸本
高176厘米 宽46.3厘米
峨眉山博物馆藏

行书"含宏大海千川受，空洞长天一鑑垂"七言联。上题"报国寺厅壁"，落款"刘孟伉"，款下钤白文"刘梦伉"、朱文"呓叟豪"两印。刘梦伉（1894～1969年），名贞健，字孟伉，四川云阳县人。现代书法家，曾任四川省文史馆馆长。

行书对联　林散之
Couplet in running script by Lin Sanzhi

纸本
高247.5厘米　宽31.2厘米
峨眉山博物馆藏

林散之，安徽和县乌江人，原名以霖，号三痴，后改名散之，别号左耳、散耳、聋叟、江上老人，为当代著名书法家、画家、诗人。林散之早年曾名"三痴"，痴诗，痴书，痴画，"散之"即由"三痴"谐音而来。晚年笔墨更是出神入化，诗中有画，画中有书，有"三绝"之誉。这幅对联为林散之82岁所写，挥洒自如，是其晚年书法佳作。

灵山铜佛
鎏金释迦牟尼铜立像
鎏金释迦牟尼铜坐像
鎏金释迦牟尼铜坐像
鎏金释迦牟尼铜坐像
鎏金释迦牟尼铜坐像
鎏金普贤菩萨铜坐像
鎏金药师佛铜坐像
鎏金释迦牟尼铜坐像
鎏金观世音铜坐像
鎏金观世音铜坐像
鎏金释迦牟尼、多宝佛并坐铜像
鎏金阿弥陀佛铜立像
鎏金阿弥陀佛铜立像
鎏金莲花观音铜坐像
鎏金木雕大势至菩萨像
鎏金阿閦玉佛坐像

峨眉山文物

佛教造像
Buddhism Statues

136-159

灵山铜佛
Lingshan Copper Buddha

西晋永安元年（305年）
通高18.5 底宽13厘米
峨眉山博物馆藏

属早期佛教造像。呈山峰形状，底边为弧形，铸有莲瓣纹，山体上饰峰峦15座，正中的峰峦上贴塑释迦佛在菩提树下成道像。释迦为正面坐像，着袒右肩袈裟。右侧峰峦上贴塑有释迦佛在菩提树下成道像。在山体正面下端刻有"一佛二菩萨二弟子"，释迦佛立于覆莲瓣圆座上，面方圆，有胡须，头上髻作圆形，项光素面无饰，身着袒右肩袈裟，右手自然下垂施与愿印。释迦牟尼佛两侧有四菩萨，作比丘像，均侧身向佛、身着袈裟。

造像背面有铭文："永安元年太岁乙丑四月十日女邑子长生氏为母敬造各山诸佛一龛永久供养。"

鎏金释迦牟尼铜立像
Gilded Standing Copper Statue of Sakyamuni

明（1368~1644年）
通高61厘米
峨眉山博物馆藏

具有浓郁藏传佛教风格。头部高高的螺髻顶部有一颗硕大圆润的宝珠，双目微闭，大耳垂肩，身着袈裟，袒露右臂和胸部，跣足立于莲台上，手施转法轮印。造型线条流畅，纹饰精美，形神皆妙。从造型风格看，深受元代阿尼哥"梵像"影响，而迥异于汉地佛像。

鎏金释迦牟尼铜坐像
Gilded Sitting Copper Statue of Sakyamuni
明（1368～1644年）
通高62.5厘米
峨眉山博物馆藏
面容丰满，螺髻高耸，身着双领下垂式袈裟，结跏趺坐于束腰莲台上，手施禅定印，双眉微闭、神态端庄。生动流畅的造型，巧妙地体现出了佛祖慈悲为怀、佛法无边的意境。

鎏金释迦牟尼铜坐像
Gilded Sitting Copper Statue of Sakyamuni
明（1368～1644年）
通高34.5厘米
峨眉山博物馆藏
造像风格深受明画家陈老莲的影响。头大身短、面容丰满、螺髻遍头、眼帘低垂，身着双领下垂式袈裟，内着天衣，手施禅定印，结跏趺坐。佛像造型创造出一种不同于唐宋时期的新样式，但佛祖慈悲庄严，风采依然。

鎏金释迦牟尼铜坐像
Gilded Sitting Copper Statue of Sakyamuni
明（1368~1644年）
通高34.5厘米
峨眉山博物馆藏
与前佛像基本相似，不同之处在于手施与愿印。

鎏金释迦牟尼铜坐像
Gilded Sitting Copper Statue of Sakyamuni
明（1368~1644年）
通高18厘米
峨眉山博物馆藏
表现佛祖苦修的造像。佛祖盘左腿坐在束腰须弥座上，面容清瘦，披衣袒胸，双手放在右膝上，头向右枕于右膝手背上，双目微闭，作沉思状。佛像鎏金，与未鎏金的须弥座区别明显。整个造型构思巧妙，别出心裁，也许是为了表示苦修的艰辛，特别在佛像嘴周围饰有胡须。

鎏金普贤菩萨铜坐像
Gilded Sitting Copper Statue of Samantabhadra Bodhisattva

明（1368~1644年）
通高19.9厘米
峨眉山博物馆藏

普贤菩萨骑白象，是宋代以后佛教造像中的普遍做法，这尊普贤菩萨亦不例外。其头戴镂空花冠、慈眉善目，着双领下垂式袈裟，胸前饰璎珞，单跏趺坐于白象上。据《法华经》，普贤菩萨曾告诉佛，若有人颂读该经，"我尔时乘六牙白象王，与大菩萨具诣其所、而自献身、供养守护、安慰其心"。此像人物造型线条流畅，白象作卧地状、通体鎏金。

鎏金药师佛铜坐像
Gilded Sitting Copper Statue of Medicine Buddha

明（1368～1644年）
通高34.5厘米
峨眉山博物馆藏

为具有尼泊尔风格的藏传佛教造像。佛头高髻再饰螺髻，双耳垂肩，微向外撇，衣着袒右通肩袈裟，露出右臂及胸，左手持钵，右手施与愿印，结跏趺坐于束腰莲台上。整个造像做工精细，尤其是面部鼻梁挺拔、鼓眼弯眉，不同于中土佛教造像。

鎏金释迦牟尼铜坐像
Gilded Sitting Copper Statue of Sakyamuni

清（1644～1911年）
通高29厘米
峨眉山博物馆藏

为藏传佛教艺术风格的佛祖造像。高高的髻上遍饰螺髻，作低头沉思状，身着袒右袈裟，结跏趺坐，造型简洁。

鎏金观世音铜坐像
Gilded Sitting Copper Statue of Avalokiteshvara Bodhisattva

清（1644～1911年）
通高36.5厘米
峨眉山博物馆藏

原造像为一对，这是其中的一尊右像，属于比较典型的民间佛教造像。观世音像面庞圆润、细眉慈目、作微笑状，头戴天冠，身着双领袈裟，袒胸露乳，腹部系扎裹肚，跣足骑坐在独角瑞兽上，姿态自然随意。瑞兽呈红色、四牛蹄形足卧地，回首顾盼。整个造型动静结合，极为生动。

鎏金观世音铜坐像
Gilded Sitting Copper Statue of Avalokiteshvara Bodhisattva

清（1644～1911年）
通高35厘米
峨眉山博物馆藏

头戴天冠，身着双领袈裟，袒胸露乳，跣足骑坐于独角瑞兽上，其造型风格与前像基本相同。唯瑞兽为青色四足，形似虎爪，显示出独具匠心之处。

Buddhism Statues
151

鎏金释迦牟尼、多宝佛并坐铜像
Gilded Side-by-Side Sitting Copper Statues of Sakyamuni and Many-Jewels Buddha

清（1644～1911年）
通高31厘米
峨眉山博物馆藏

据《妙法莲华经》"见宝塔品"记载，当释迦牟尼在讲《法华经》时，忽然地下涌出安置多宝佛全身舍利的塔现于空中。于是，释迦牟尼告诉诸天菩萨、这宝塔中有如来全身，乃是过去东方世界宝净国土的佛，号为多宝。释迦还在诸天菩萨的悬请下，开启塔门，示现多宝佛身。此时，多宝佛于宝塔中让出半座，说"释迦牟尼佛，可就此座"。于是释迦欣然入塔，与多宝佛共同结跏趺坐，宣讲经义。该尊造像就生动地再现了这一情景：释迦牟尼手施禅定印、多宝佛施说法印、二佛皆结跏趺坐，身着双领下垂式袈裟，内着天衣，袒露右胸，座下是三层楼阁，其内遍坐诸天菩萨，象征着多宝佛居住的宝净国土。

鎏金阿弥陀佛铜立像
Gilded Standing Copper Statue of Amitabha Buddha

清（1644～1911年）
通高31.5厘米
峨眉山博物馆藏

阿弥陀佛是佛教艺术喜见的题材之一。该像头饰螺髻，脸部丰颐，身着双领下垂式袈裟，左手置于胸前，右手施与愿印，立于束腰莲台上。值得注意的是，佛像的白毫相不在眉心、而置于头顶脑门中央，并饰朱彩。

鎏金阿弥陀佛铜像立像
Gilded Standing Copper Statue of Amitabha Buddha

清（1644～1911年）
通高43.5厘米
峨眉山博物馆藏

看似比例不甚协调的阿弥陀佛，面容丰满，身着袒右通肩袈裟，露出右臂与胸部双乳，左手托莲朵于身前，右手施与愿印，头部螺髻上戴一葫芦状宝刹，与汉地佛教造像不甚相同，别具匠心。

鎏金莲花观音铜坐像
Gilded Sitting Copper Statue of Avalokiteshvara Bodhisattva with Lotus

清（1644～1911年）
通高7.5厘米
峨眉山博物馆藏

具有明显的藏传佛教艺术风格。头戴莲花冠，身饰璎珞，袒胸露乳，细腰、清秀俊美，结跏趺坐在莲台上。两臂旁伸出的莲花，象征着佛国的净土世界。

鎏金木雕大势至菩萨像
Gilded Wood-carved Statue of Mahasthamaprapta Bodhisattva

清（1644～1911年）
通高23.5厘米
峨眉山博物馆藏

在佛教造像中，鎏金木雕佛像相对较少。这尊鎏金木雕大势至菩萨具有铜像一般的质感，头饰双髻，戴三角佛冠，面容圆润，神态自若，造型秀美。身着双领下垂式袈裟，手持莲枝，跣足立于束腰莲台上。

鎏金阿閦玉佛坐像
Gilded Sitting Jade Statue of Aksobhya Buddha

清（1644～1911年）
通高45厘米
峨眉山博物馆藏

佛教密宗造像，是金刚界五智如来中的东方如来。按密宗教义，金刚界是体现大日如来"智德"的，共有五种智德，并为教化众生而化为五方五佛，其中东方阿閦佛就代表了大圆镜智，亦明金刚智。佛像慈目含笑，头饰螺髻，身着袒右通肩袈裟，左手执于腹前，右手自然下垂成触地印。该像原通体鎏金，现仅在衣褶处残存鎏金。全像为整块缅甸玉雕成，玉质精美，弥足珍贵。

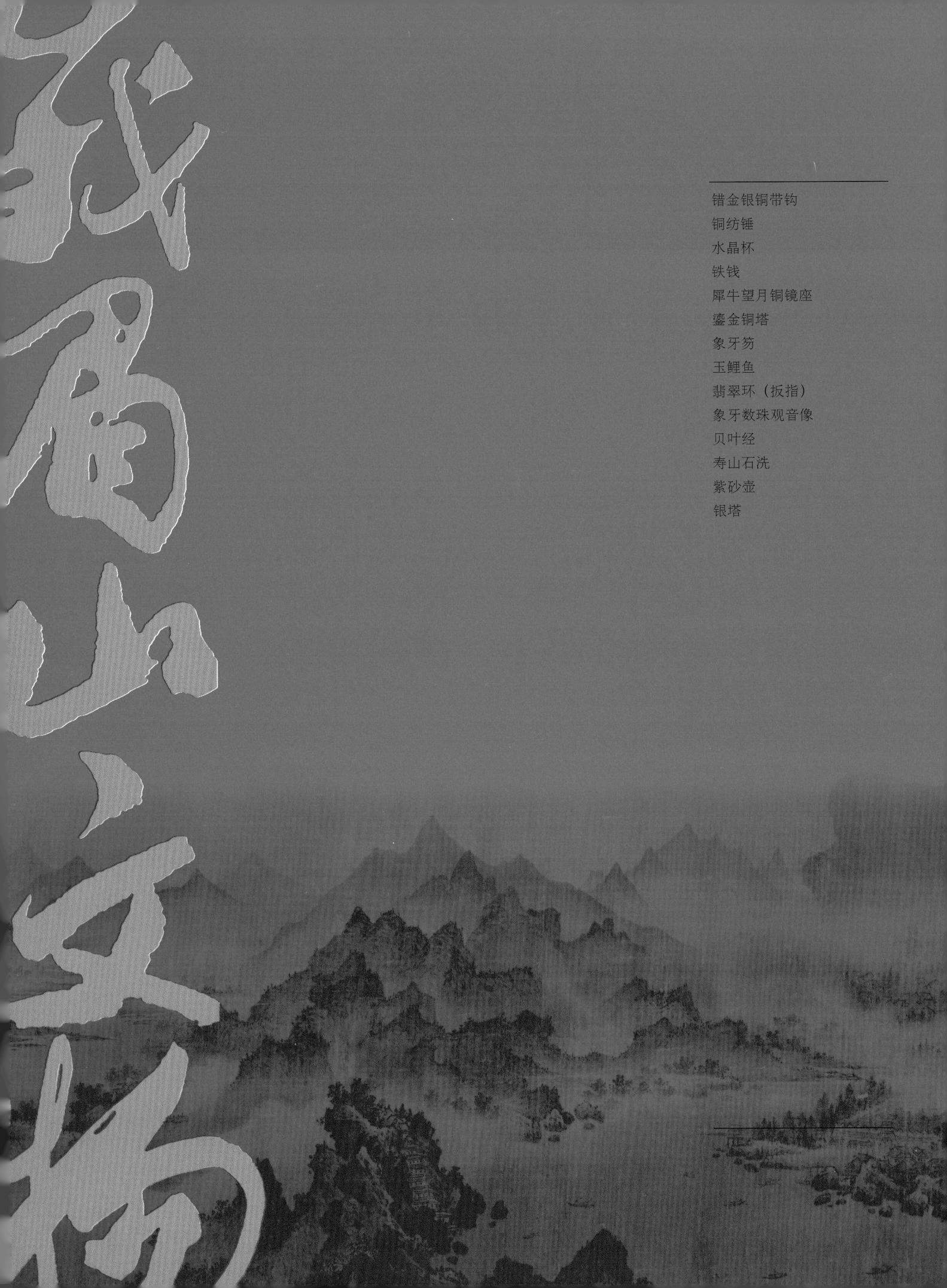

错金银铜带钩
铜纺锤
水晶杯
铁钱
犀牛望月铜镜座
鎏金铜塔
象牙笏
玉鲤鱼
翡翠环（扳指）
象牙数珠观音像
贝叶经
寿山石洗
紫砂壶
银塔

峨眉山文物

杂件
Miscellaneous

160-177

错金银铜带钩
Gold & Silver Decorated Copper Belt
战国（前475年～前221年）
通长17厘米
峨眉山博物馆藏
下端有钉柱，用于钉住皮带的一头。上端曲首作钩，钩似蛇首。身修长呈棒状，内弧。饰错金银漩涡纹、菱形纹和几何纹，显示出古蜀工匠精湛的工艺水平。

铜纺锤
Copper spindle
战国（前475年～前221年）
通高19厘米
身呈喇叭塔状，分三段，圆锥形尖，中间有凸棱六个，底端呈圆瓶形，应是一种实用的生产工具。

水晶杯
Crystal cup
唐—宋（618～1279年）
通高3.3厘米 口径6.2厘米
足径2.8厘米 重53.31克
峨眉山市文物管理所藏
天然水晶琢成，属烟晶质。六葵瓣形缘、敞口、圆唇、六弧形斜腹、圜底、圈足。外壁近口沿处各有一横向凹槽。此杯是四川地区宋代窖藏中首次出土具有晚唐风格的珍贵文物，对研究唐宋时期水晶制造工艺提供了实物资料。

铁 钱
Iron coin

宋（960～1279年）
峨眉山市文物管理所藏
2002年8月出土于峨眉山市罗目镇，总重量达16.32吨，有约160万枚铁钱。计有北宋元祐、崇宁、大观、政和、宣和、靖康；南宋绍兴、隆兴、庆元、嘉定、宝庆等年号。是目前我国同一地点出土铁钱最多的一处，有"中国第一钱山"之称。

犀牛望月铜镜座
Copper Mirror Seat of Rhinoceros Viewing the Moon

明（1368～1644年）
通高16.7厘米
峨眉山博物馆藏
牛左前肢跪地，右前肢伸展，为半卧状。独角前伸、双耳直竖、嘴紧闭、眼微睁、回首仰视、神态安详。背上有鞍，鞍上竖月牙形镜座。

鎏金铜塔
Gilded copper pagoda

明（1368～1644年）
通高53厘米
峨眉山博物馆藏

塔身楼阁式，六面九级，其上宝刹缺失。楼阁下有浮雕一佛二菩萨坐像，身后有火焰纹头光。座下为二力士，束腰须弥座中央有三身坐佛。整个佛塔俊秀挺拔，是塔似庙，应对了佛教"塔寺一体、塔在中央"的旧制。

象牙笏
Ivory Tablet
明（1368～1644年）
长54.4厘米
峨眉山博物馆藏
笏也称"手板"，古代大臣上朝觐见时手中所执。此笏用象牙制作而成，光滑细润，色橙黄。狭长形、上大下小，侧微弧。

玉鲤鱼
Jade Cyprinus Carpio
清（1644～1911年）
长8.5厘米
峨眉山博物馆藏
玉质莹润、色灰白。鱼阔体扁身，嘴微张，背鳍高凸，前鳍贴身，后鳍由两侧向上分开，尾扇形上翘呈游动状。腮处钻有小孔以穿绳，雕刻细腻，栩栩如生。

翡翠环（扳指）
Sapphire ring (Banzhi)
清（1644～1911年）
高2.3厘米
峨眉山博物馆藏
清代墓葬出土。玉质莹润、色翠绿。呈管状。

Miscellaneous
169

象牙数珠观音像
Guanyin Statue Holding Ivory Beads
清（1644~1911年）
通高10.3厘米
峨眉山博物馆藏

为民间艺人依据佛教密宗经典创造的一件观音菩萨像。身穿交领袈裟，左手持念珠于膝，右手覆其上。按照佛教中的说法，数珠不仅在诵念佛经时用来计数，更能消除魔障、增长功德。此像神态慈祥，给人以亲切之感。

贝叶经
Beiye Scripture
清（1644~1911年）
通高4.5厘米
峨眉山博物馆藏

贝叶，是贝多罗树的叶片。贝多罗树属南印度、缅甸和斯里兰卡常见的一种阔叶棕榈树，其叶长肥厚实，用于写经的须有八年以上树龄，经过处理后用铁笔刻写，再用墨汁涂抹，凉干后用线串起，再装入箧中，为寺庙中的镇寺之宝。该贝页经内容为《法华经》。

寿山石洗
Shoushan Stonewash

民国（1912～1949年）
通高7.6厘米
峨眉山博物馆藏

寿山石雕刻，呈血红色。口沿桃形、深腹，柄部透雕、连接洗底部。腹下部接柄处饰高浮雕花瓣。

紫砂壶
Purple Gray Tea Pot

民国（1912～1949年）
通高20厘米
峨眉山博物馆藏

壶酱红色，椭圆形壶身，藤枝状提梁，梁前部分双枝塑于藤枝状曲流两侧壶肩上。弧形圆盖、扣齿、藤枝状盖纽，纽上有孔，可穿细绳与梁相连。壶身正面刻行草铭文两行，为："凤茶孙儿贮，尾浮鹅酒黄。"落款为："天梵吾师赐玩 受业 佩聪敬赠"。壶身背面刻喜雀踏梅。在壶盖内刻有"恺大"两字。做工精美、紫砂细腻，为紫砂壶中的精品。

银塔

Silver Pagoda

民国（1911—1949年）
通高35.5厘米
峨眉山博物馆藏

纯银打制，六面七级，楼阁式，逐级向上收分，每面檐沿下悬一风铃。此塔时代虽晚，铸造却颇具特色。塔身后面刻有铭文"峨山锡瓦店 普贤大帝位前 隆昌县众善民 敬赠 荣华银楼制 民国卅七年五月敬立"，具有一定的资料价值。

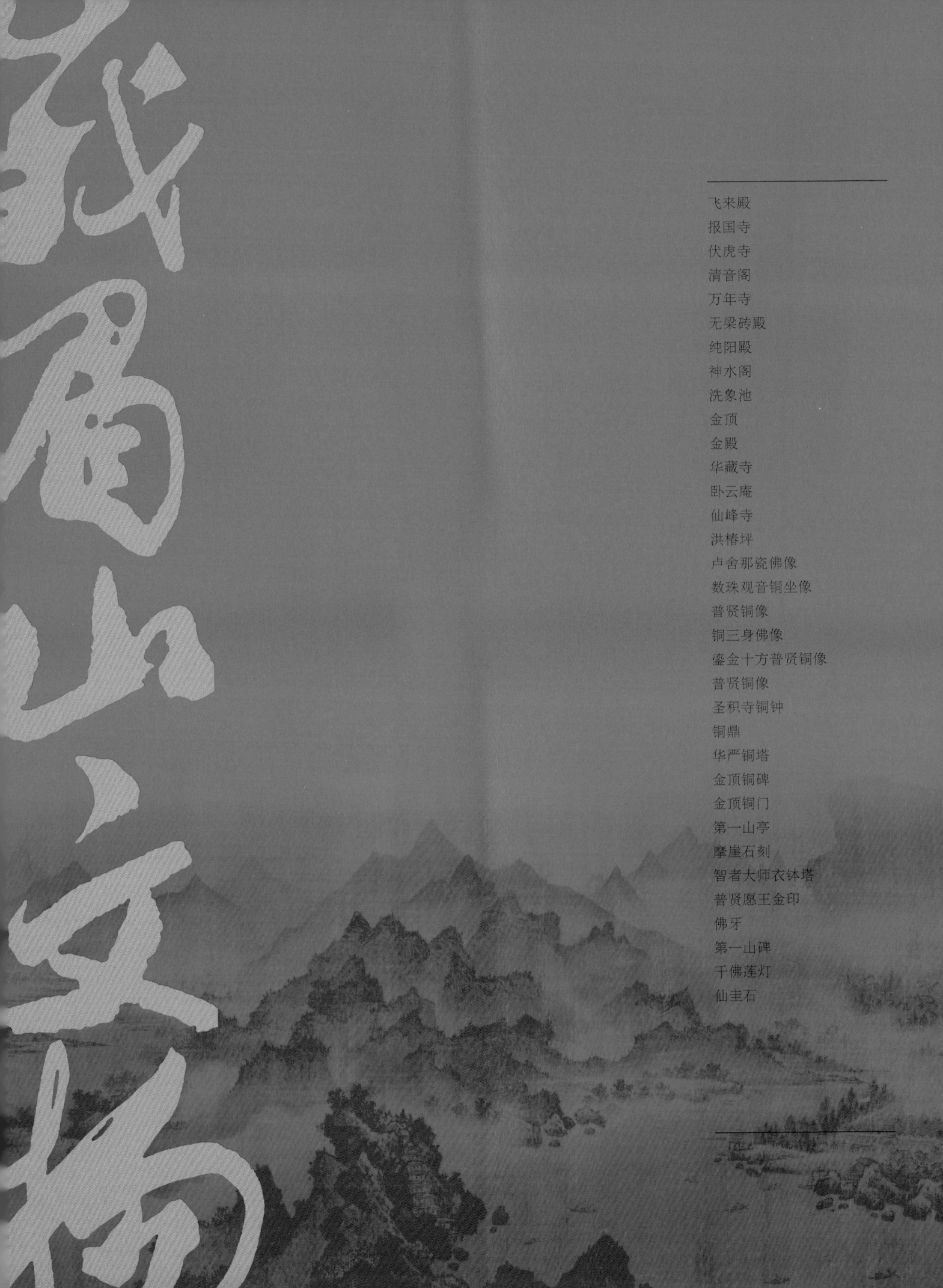

飞来殿
报国寺
伏虎寺
清音阁
万年寺
无梁砖殿
纯阳殿
神水阁
洗象池
金顶
金殿
华藏寺
卧云庵
仙峰寺
洪椿坪
卢舍那瓷佛像
数珠观音铜坐像
普贤铜像
铜三身佛像
鎏金十方普贤铜像
普贤铜像
圣积寺铜钟
铜鼎
华严铜塔
金顶铜碑
金顶铜门
第一山亭
摩崖石刻
智者大师衣钵塔
普贤愿王金印
佛牙
第一山碑
千佛莲灯
仙圭石

峨眉山文物

寺庙建筑及其他
Monasteries and Others

178-219

飞来殿
Feilai Hall

始建于北宋淳化四年（993年），后因失修损毁。元至元十六年（1279年）复建。平面布局为檐柱三开间，内柱五开间，上施斗拱、昂翼承托内柱下平槫，据前上昂出象鼻形卷昂，下昂出龙首，雕刻细致生动。盘旋于当心柱上的两条泥塑盘龙栩栩如生。

报国寺
Baoguo Monastery

原名会宗堂。明万历四十三年明光道人创建，供奉着佛、道、儒三教的代表人物。清初迁建于现址，由康熙御题"报国寺"匾额而易名。寺占地近4万平方米，坐西向东，殿宇五重，依次为山门、弥勒殿、大雄殿、七佛殿、藏经楼，倚山因势，逐级升高，具有浓郁的四川庭院式民居风格。

伏虎寺
Fuhu Monastery

清（1644～1911年）
位于伏虎岭下

初创于晋时，宋代称龙神堂，清顺治八年至康熙十年（1651～1671年）重建。建筑布局采用复四合院与散点分布相结合，面积近两万平方米。中轴线上有天王殿、普贤殿、大雄殿，南侧有华严铜塔亭，北侧有罗汉堂，西建御书楼。整个建筑群掩映于繁茂的林木之中，因此有"密林藏伏虎"之称。

清音阁
Qingyin Pavilion
明—清（1368～1911年）
位于峨眉山牛心岭下
唐代为牛心寺（又名卧云寺），明初广济禅师更名清音阁。以清音阁为中心，纵横约4平方公里，亭台楼桥坐落于山水林石之间，相映成趣，称为"双桥清音"，是峨眉山著名景观之一。

万年寺
Wannian Monastery
明—清（1368~1911年）
位于峨眉山观心岭下

创建于东晋，名普贤寺。唐代改称白水寺、宋代名白水普贤寺。北宋太平兴国年间，宋太宗遣使铸造普贤骑象巨型铜像供奉寺内。明万历年间建无梁砖殿，明神宗御题"圣寿万年寺"。现存殿宇五重，分别为山门、弥勒殿、砖殿、巍峨宝殿和大雄宝殿。寺周群峰环抱，每至秋季，红叶迎风翻飞，白水山影横斜，称为"白水秋风"，是峨眉山十景之一。

无梁砖殿
Beamless Brick Hall
明（1368~1644年）
位于万年寺内

建于明万历二十九年（1601年）。单体布局，体近正方，顶呈覆釜，为石基砖拱无梁殿。通高17.12米，面阔15.97米，进深16.06米，建筑面积257平方米。殿内存有北宋普贤骑象巨型铜像。四百多年来，经历了5~7.9级地震18次，仍完好无损，堪称我国古代建筑史上的奇迹。

纯阳殿
Chunyang Hall

明—清（1368~1911年）
位于峨眉山赤城峰下
宋时为新峨眉观，明万历乙酉年（1585年）重建，名吕仙行祠。崇祯六年（1633年）增修，更名为纯阳吕祖殿，供奉吕洞宾像。后道士离去，僧人居之。清初，增修新殿及静室，供奉普贤大士。

神水阁
Shenshui Pavilion

1992年重建
位于峨眉山皇帽峰下
原为明代巡抚吴用先别墅。阁前有玉液神泉，故名神水阁，又名圣水阁。现有殿宇四重，分别为观音殿、弥勒殿、大雄殿和普贤殿。

洗象池
Xixiang (Elephant washing) Pond
清（1644～1911年）
位于峨眉山钻天坡上
创建于明正德年间，名初喜亭，清康熙三十八年（1699年）扩建为大寺，名天花禅院。传说普贤骑象登山，曾在此用水洗象，故名洗象池。现存有弥勒殿、大雄宝殿、观音殿及藏经楼、客寮等。每当月夜，云收雾敛，满天清晖，恰似人间广寒，誉称"象池夜月"。

金顶
Jinding
海拔3079.3米，是峨眉山的主峰，又名光明之顶、幸福之顶。这里是世界上著名的佛教朝拜圣地，也是世界上最壮观的天然观景台。站在金顶上远望，层层峰峦簇拥脚下，东可望青衣江、大渡河、岷江，西可望白雪皑皑的贡嘎雪山，可充分体会到"云上金顶"的绝妙。

Monasteries and Others

金 殿
Golden Hall

2005年重建

1602年始建，由妙峰禅师募造。因此殿的瓦、柱、门、窗等皆铜质渗金，阳光照耀之下，金光灿烂，故名为金殿。清末毁于火灾，2005年重建。

华藏寺
Huazang Monastery
位于峨眉山主峰金顶

始建于东汉,称普光殿,唐宋改称光相寺。明万历年间(1573~1619年)妙峰禅师在殿后最高处营建铜殿。清末毁于火。2005年,华藏寺按历史面貌复建,由金殿和大雄宝殿组成。金殿采用金瓦,大雄宝殿采用铜瓦,梁栓、门窗、斗拱等均为铜铸。两殿均在中轴线上,渐次升高。尤其金殿外观形象给人以崇高而神秘之感,达到了超尘除俗、俯视凡界的宗教意境。游人步入其中,有渐入天国之感。

卧云庵
Woyun Nunnery
明—清(1368~1911年)
位于峨眉山主峰金顶

初建于唐,明嘉靖年间性天和尚重建,因寺周常白云环绕,故名卧云。明末倾圮,清康熙年间可闻禅师重建,因顶覆锡瓦,故又名银殿。今银装素裹的卧云庵与金殿、铜殿相互辉映于金顶之上。

仙峰寺
Xianfeng Monastery

清（1644～1911年）
位于峨眉山仙峰岩下

创建于明初，名仙峰禅院或称天峰禅院。因附近有九老洞，故俗称九老洞。万历四十年（1612年）扩建、明末烧毁。清乾隆年间再建，现存弥勒殿、大雄宝殿、舍利宝殿、餐秀山房等。寺宇屋面全为锡瓦、铝皮所盖，衬托于浓翠欲滴的苍藤古树之中。寺周深卉长林、烟云缭绕、蒙岩幽壑，誉称"九老仙府"。

Monasteries and Others

洪椿坪
Hongchunping

清（1644～1911年）
位于峨眉山天池峰下
因寺前有洪椿古树而得名，亦名千佛禅院。传为晋时宝掌和尚结茅处，现存建筑大部为清乾隆四十七年至五十五年所建。寺周古木扶疏，群峰如黛，云雾空濛，翠沾人衣，誉称"洪椿晓雨"，为峨眉山十景之一。

卢舍那瓷佛像
Porcelain Figure of Vairochana Buddha

明（1368～1644年）
通高2.47米
现供奉于峨眉山北瓷佛寺
明永乐十三年（1415年），江西景德镇瓷商谢元芳、田万鳌发愿塑烧。佛端坐千叶莲花之上，身着千佛莲衣，象征《梵网经》中的"一花一世界，千叶千如来"。

数珠观音铜坐像
Ivory Guanyin Holding Beads

南宋（1127~1279年）
通高1.3米
现供奉于峨眉山白龙洞
此像铸造于南宋，为峨眉山较早的佛教造像之一。观音单跏趺坐、头戴花冠，胸部饰璎珞，左手持念珠，右手抚膝。

普贤铜像
Copper Statue of Puxian

北宋（960~1127年）
现供奉于万年寺砖殿内
佛像包括1尊普贤骑象铜像、24尊圆觉铁像、303尊小铁佛像等，共计328尊铜铁造像。铸造于北宋太平兴国五年（980年）。其中普贤骑象铜像通高7.35米，重约62吨。普贤佛像通体鎏金，盘坐于六牙象背负莲花座上。头带双层五佛金冠，两眼微合，唇角稍敛，袒胸饰璎珞，身披袈裟，右手执金如意，左手置胸前，手心向上。六牙象背饰雕鞍，彩带辔头，四蹄遒劲有力，卷鼻舒尾，似将远行，富有动感。各部比例匀称，煅铸工艺精湛，整个造像采用分块焊接而成，代表了北宋时期金属铸造工艺的最高水平。

铜三身佛像
Three-body Copper Buddha Statue

明（1368～1644年）
通高3.85米
现供奉于万年寺大雄殿内

三身佛像分为"法身"、"报身"、"应身"，为明嘉靖十三年（1534年）别传和尚铸造。三像造型精美、体态均称，是明代铜铸佛像中的翘楚之作。

鎏金十方普贤铜像
Ten-heads Copper Statue of Puxian Buddha

通高48米 重660吨
2005年建于峨眉山金顶

位于金顶的的鎏金十方普贤铜像流光溢彩，美仑美奂。佛像共有十个头像，体现着普贤十大行愿的内涵。智行广大遍十方的普贤，寄托着人间的美好愿望。

鎏金十方普贤铜佛像是世界上最高的佛造像，由台座和十方普贤像组成。其中台座高6米，边长27米，四面刻有普贤的十种广大行愿。整个佛像设计完美、工艺流畅，堪称铜铸巨佛的旷世之作，具有很高的文化价值和观赏审美价值，是海峡两岸艺术家心灵的碰撞，智慧的结晶。

普贤铜像
Copper Statue of Puxian

清（1644～1911年）
通高1.2米
现供奉于金顶华藏寺金殿
普贤菩萨结跏趺坐于三层仰莲台上，其下是白象。普贤菩萨头戴高冠，身着双领下垂式袈裟，胸前饰缨珞，双手执如意，慈祥端庄。

圣积寺铜钟
Copper Bell of Shengji Monastery

明（1368～1644年）
通高2.4米 直径2.2米 重12500公斤
位于报国寺凤凰堡
明嘉靖四十三年（1564年）慧宗别传禅师募资铸造。钟口状若莲瓣，向外微张。有"巴蜀钟王"之称。

铜鼎
Copper Tripod

明（1368～1644年）
通高1.2米 口径0.77米
现藏万年寺

为明代嘉靖元年（1522年）无为和尚铸造。鼎身铸有高浮雕云龙图案，三足，为狮面龙爪握珠形。

华严铜塔
Huayan Copper Pagoda

元（1271～1368年）
通高5.8米
现供奉于伏虎寺

塔门上铸有"南无阿弥陀佛华严宝塔"10字。为八面十四层，紫铜铸造。塔身铸有佛像4700尊及《华严经》全文。造像大多为高浮雕，主题感很强、佛像、菩萨等均突出于壁面，雕饰富丽，堪称中国古代艺术的精品。

金顶铜碑
Jinding Copper Tablet

明（1368~1644年）
高1.78米 宽0.8米 厚0.17米
现藏金顶华藏寺金殿
为明万历年间（1573~1619年）妙峰禅师修建金殿时所铸。正面刻王毓宗撰集王羲之字《大峨山永明华藏寺新建铜殿记》，背面刻傅光宅撰集诸遂良字《峨眉山普贤金殿碑》。

金顶铜门
Jinding Copper Door

明（1368～1644年）
每扇高1.95米 宽0.45米
现藏金顶华藏寺金殿

铸造于明成化壬寅年（1482年）。原系华藏寺铜殿构件。清光绪十六年（1892年）铜殿毁于火，仅存铜门四扇。门上铸有高浮雕佛像88尊，下部铸有鱼、龙、麒麟、凤等浮雕图案，造型生动，具有较高的观赏价值。

Monasteries and Others
211

第一山亭
No.1 Mount Pavilion

2005年建
亭高16.1米
位于峨眉山登山步行道入口广场
这里是进入峨眉山的起点，为中国目前最大的铜亭。亭重檐翘角，精工巧构，气宇轩昂，金碧辉煌。其上悬有四匾，分别为"第一山"、"峨眉山"、"大光明山"、"皇人之山"。亭中间有"水浮莲花托起晶莹宝石"，高2.5米，宽1米。"宝石"内镶嵌铜铸"世界遗产"和"国家级风景名胜区"标志。

摩崖石刻
Cliff Carving

2005年建
位于峨眉山登山步行道入口
崖石上刻有"神州第一山"和"山之领袖"9个朱色大字。四周分别刻有名人名言，代表了魏晋、元、明、清不同朝代，不同人物对峨眉山的评价。

智者大师衣钵塔
Clothing Pagoda of Master Wisdom
明（1368～1644年）
通高6.1米
位于神水阁正殿前
隋智者大师因礼普贤，驻锡峨眉山中峰寺。明万历年间建大师衣钵塔，以志其事。塔共7层，用石雕砌，实心，檐角高啄，上层尚存佛像4尊，下两层有二龙戏珠、莲花等浮雕图案。

普贤愿王金印
Golden Chop of Puxian
明（1368～1644年）
边长11.5厘米
现藏万年寺
此印系明万历皇帝朱翊钧敕建峨眉山普贤砖殿时钦赐。印为正方形，印面正中篆刻"普贤愿王之宝"，上方刻楷书"大明万历"，左边刻"御题砖殿"，右边刻"敕赐峨山"。

佛牙
Buddha Tooth
明（1368～1644年）
长44厘米 重6.5公斤
现藏万年寺
为明嘉靖年间锡兰（今斯里兰卡）友人所赠。经鉴定为距今约60万年的剑齿象化石。

第一山碑
No.1 Mountain Tablet

高2.35米 宽0.95米 厚0.22米
位于万年寺山门内左侧
北宋书法家米芾书，纵横变化，雄健清新，俨然有腾龙卧虎之势。

千佛莲灯
Thousand-Buddha Lotus Lamp

1928年
通高1.1米 直径0.7米
现藏洪椿坪
这件莲灯是重庆雕工花三年时间精制而成。灯体雕塑有佛像和神像320余尊，并在7个翘角上塑有形态生动的云龙神兽。图像形成多组佛道故事。佛道之争，历来水火难容，但在此盏莲灯上却相容共处，十分有趣。

仙圭石（下页）
Xian Gui Stone

仙峰寺前面有一巨大的摩岩石刻，上面刻有"南无普贤菩萨"，为泸州周祚章书写，字体浑厚端庄，颇讲法度。顶端因有赵熙所书"仙圭"二字，故称"仙圭石"。

附录 \ 峨眉山古迹分布图
Attachments \ Distribution of Historic Relics in Mt. Emei

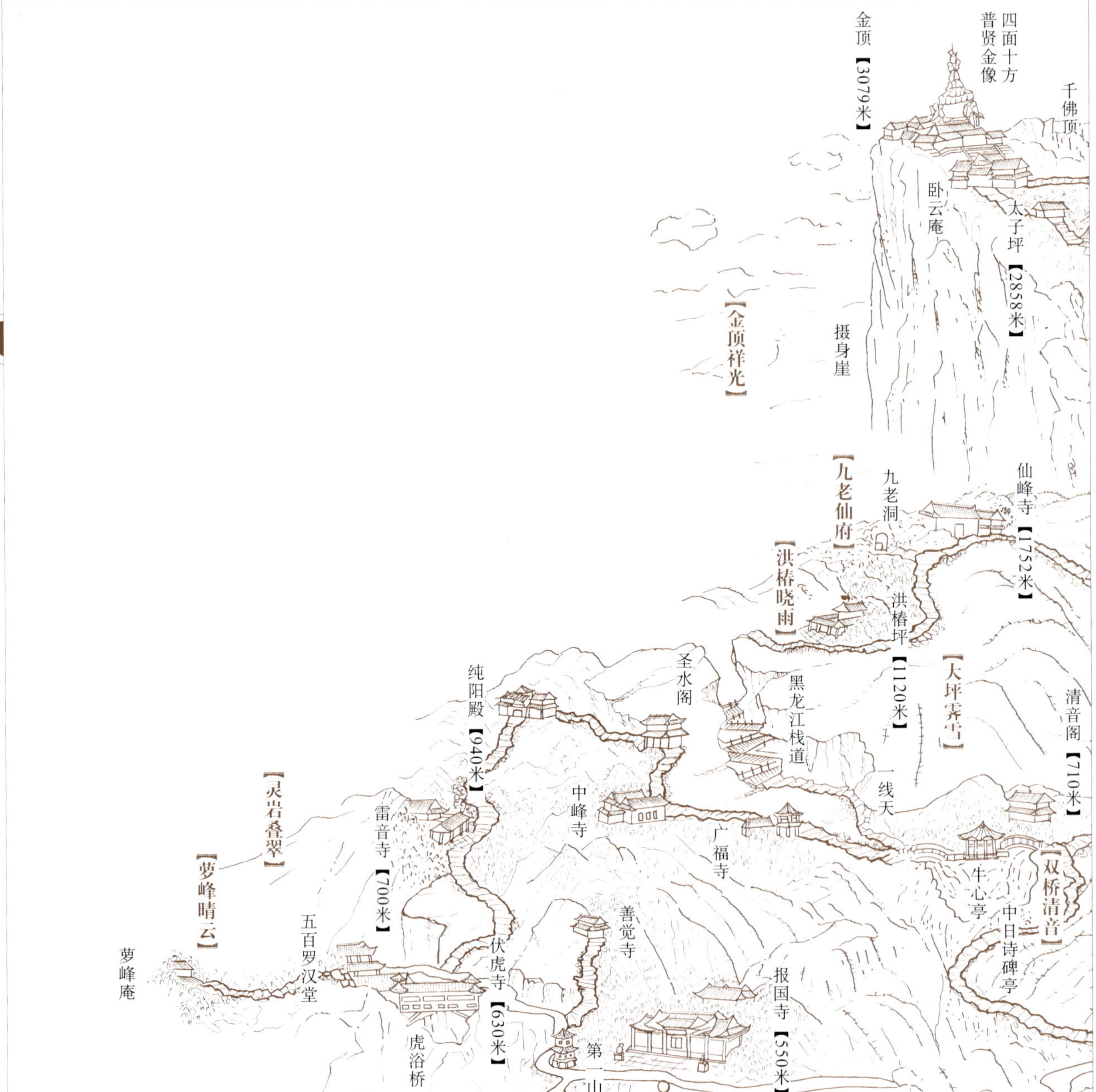

- 千佛顶
- 四面十方普贤金像
- 金顶【3079米】
- 卧云庵
- 太子坪【2858米】
- 摄身崖
- 【金顶祥光】
- 仙峰寺【1752米】
- 九老洞
- 【九老仙府】
- 洪椿坪
- 【洪椿晓雨】
- 清音阁【710米】
- 洪椿坪【1120米】
- 【大坪霁雪】
- 黑龙江栈道
- 一线天
- 【双桥清音】
- 纯阳殿【940米】
- 圣水阁
- 牛心亭
- 中日诗碑亭
- 中峰寺
- 广福寺
- 雷音寺【700米】
- 善觉寺
- 【灵岩叠翠】
- 五百罗汉堂
- 伏虎寺【630米】
- 报国寺【550米】
- 【萝峰晴云】
- 萝峰庵
- 虎浴桥
- 第一山亭
- 【圣积晚钟】
- 天下名山牌坊
- 峨秀湖

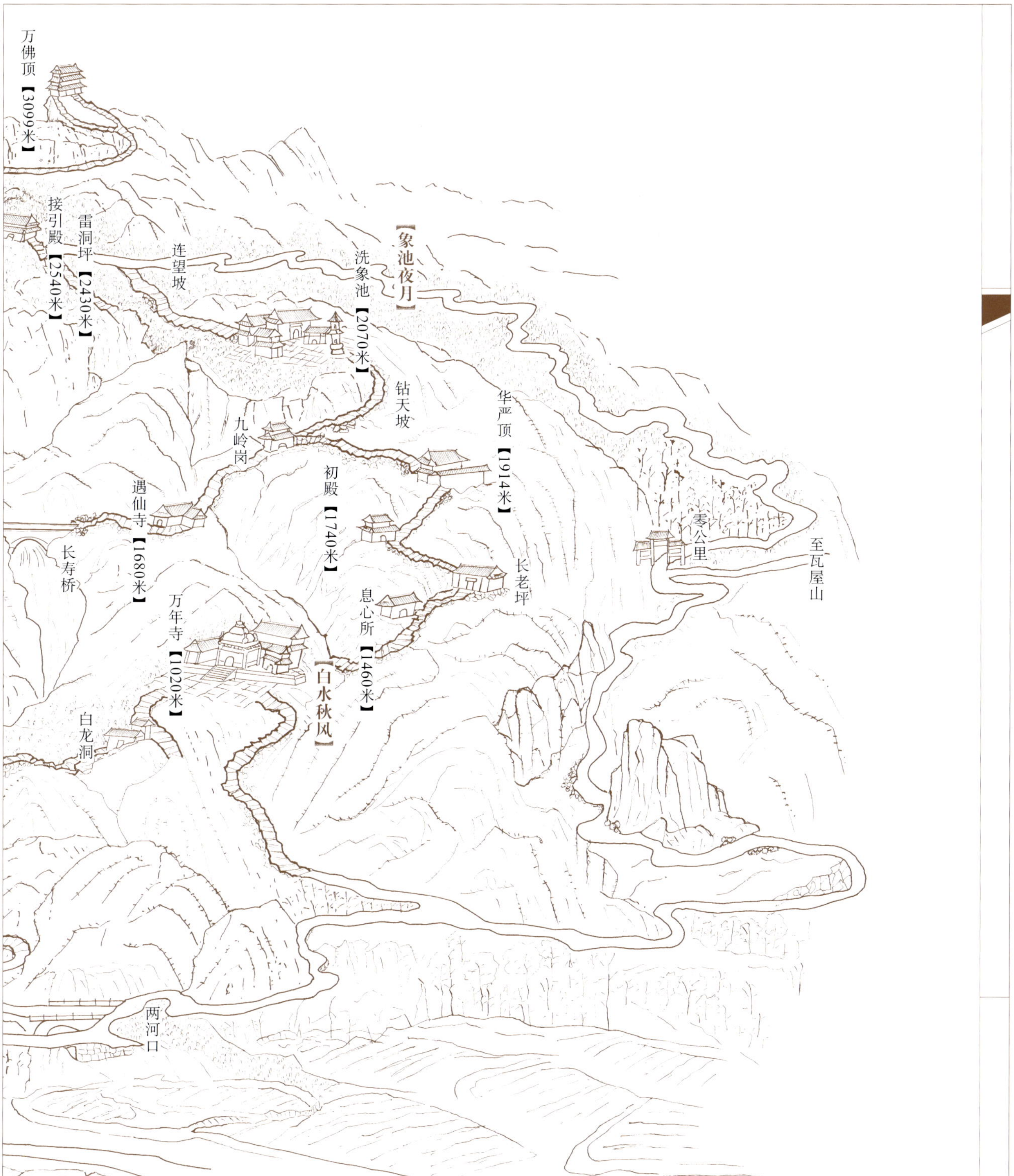
万佛顶【3099米】
接引殿【2540米】
雷洞坪【2430米】
连望坡
【象池夜月】
洗象池【2070米】
钻天坡
华严顶【1914米】
九岭岗
初殿【1740米】
遇仙寺【1680米】
长寿桥
零公里
至瓦屋山
长老坪
息心所【1460米】
万年寺【1020米】
【白水秋风】
白龙洞
两河口

附录 \ 峨眉山大事记
Attachments \ Chronicle Events of Mt. Emei

公元前1066年~公元62年

- 约西周中叶，杜宇自立为蜀王，号称望帝，峨眉山为其所辖。
- 公元前515~前488年，楚昭王曾遣使往聘楚士陆通，出领江南地。使者去，通变姓易名，游历名山大川，后隐蜀峨眉。其结庐处，位于中峰寺左里许。宋黄庭坚来游命名为"歌凤台"。
- 战国时，鬼谷先生，姓王名诩，著《珞琭子》一书于峨眉山洞（见《隋书》），至今山中雷洞坪下尚有鬼谷洞。
- 传有白衣衫者，号动灵，仿山猴动作创编"峨眉通臂拳"。
- 汉武帝建元六年（前135年），置犍为郡，峨眉山归南安县。

公元63年~公元265年

- 东汉和帝时，阴长生写《丹经》四通，一通以黄金之简刻而书之，封以白银之函，置蜀绥山（即今二峨山）。
- 永和六年（141年），五斗米道创立者张陵，作道书《灵宝》、《天官章本》等24种，中含《峨眉山神异记》3卷。
- 东汉献帝建安三年（198年），张陵之孙张鲁，在张陵所立的二十四治基础上，新增"八品游治"，其中第一治即"峨眉治"。

公元265年~公元589年

- 北魏拓跋珪登国九年（394年），益州僧明果，自长安谒印度僧竺法护回蜀上峨眉山，住锡白岩中峰之下，改乾明观为中峰寺。
- 东晋隆安年间，传高僧肇公（384~414年）开建道场于黑水寺，后称峨眉祖堂。
- 东晋安帝义熙八年（412年）高僧慧远之弟慧持来山兴建普贤寺。一说，东晋恭帝元熙二年（420年）始建普贤寺（今万年寺）。
- 北魏郦道元《水经注》中引《益州记》："平乡江东迳峨眉山，在南安县界，去成都南千里。然秋日清澄，望见两山相峙如峨眉焉。"
- 魏晋间，中印度僧宝掌入蜀礼普贤，初住今峨眉山麓灵岩寺处，后结茅于洪椿坪右峰，现名宝掌峰。
- 西晋时，西域僧阿婆多罗尊者，来礼峨眉，建道场。山高无瓦填覆，且雪雨寒薄，冻裂不坚，以木皮盖殿，故时称木皮殿。后更名化城寺、大乘寺。

公元589年~公元960年

- 隋唐之际,我国古代著名医药学家孙思邈来山采药、炼丹、著述。其《千金要方》、《千金翼方》、《孙真人丹经》等著作,均在此期间写成。
- 隋大业十一年(615年),立绥山县于峨眉山下,隶属眉山郡。
- 唐武德九年(626年),开建牛心寺于牛心岭下。
- 唐圣历年间,陈子昂自京还乡来游,著《感遇诗》38首。诗中有"浩然坐何慕,吾蜀有峨眉","飞飞骑羊子,胡乃在峨眉"等句。
- 唐开元十年(722年),一说开元十二年,李白游峨眉、青城,以居峨眉最久,作《登峨眉山》诗。
- 唐大历十一年(770年),华严宗四祖澄观来峨眉山礼普贤,登险陟高,备观圣像,著《普贤行愿品疏》。
- 唐乾符年间,敕赐晋僧肇开创之峨眉祖堂为永明华藏寺。
- 唐僖宗时,僧元安法嗣慧通来峨,望山峰奇异,重兴六寺,即归云寺、集云寺、卧云寺、黑水寺、白水寺、慧续尼院。
- 唐僧昌福、达道,在古心坪下建华严寺。

公元960年~公元1279年

- 北宋乾德、开宝年间,白水普贤寺最隆盛,朝廷设提点,驻节寺中。
- 北宋太平兴国元年(976年),宋太宗赵匡义书"天皇真人论道之地,楚狂接舆隐逸之乡"联敕赐光相寺。
- 北宋太平兴国五年(980年)二月,白水寺僧茂真奉诏入朝,太宗赐诗美之。即归,重兴白水、华严、中峰、牛心、黑水、灵岩6寺。又敕内侍张仁赞往成都,铸金铜普贤大士像,高二丈六尺,奉安于嘉州峨眉山白水普贤寺,建高阁以覆之。
- 北宋仁宗嘉祐七年(1062年)十月七日,仁宗赵祯下《发愿御书》赐白水普贤寺。
- 南宋绍兴年间,行僧心庵建伏虎寺,以镇虎患,故名。
- 南宋绍兴年间,诗僧怀古,于长老坪左万寿坡下,建殿供古佛蒲公像。明正德六年始名"万寿堂"。
- 南宋隆兴初年,洪忠宣著《嘉州江心记》载国朝太祖(宗)、仁宗、真宗赐经百卷、七宝冠、金珠璎珞袈裟各一置牛心寺。
- 南宋隆兴时,伏虎寺僧慧远,奉诏入朝,孝宗赵昚赐号佛海。
- 南宋孝宗淳熙四年(1177年)六月十九日至二十三日,范成大来山游览,撰有大量诗文。其中《峨眉山行纪》一文为现存游峨记中年代最早者,虽千字,然地理大略可考。
- 南宋淳熙十年(1183年),孝宗赵昚在东宫榜书"别峰"二字,敕赐峨眉山香山寺(即径山寺)僧别峰。香山寺当时为入山首寺。
- 南宋淳祐年间,僧绍才,重建卧云寺,复称牛心寺。
- 宋嘉洲刺史王良弼,奏请准建放光寺于顶峰之西。

公元1279年～公元1368年

- 元天顺元年（1328年），创建慈延寺，亦名仙峰寺，俗称九老洞。
- 元时建大峨楼于象牙坡上（即清初复建之灵官楼）。
- 元时，永川万华轩施造华严铜塔一合，至于圣积寺，现存于伏虎寺"华严宝塔"亭内。

公元1368年～公元1644年

- 明洪武元年（1368年），中峰寺毁于兵燹。
  同年，僧楚山开建千佛禅院于洪椿坪。明德心禅师法嗣锐峰相继修建历20余年始成。
- 明洪武十一年（1378年），太祖朱元璋遣国师宝昙重建光相寺，以铁为瓦，故俗称铁瓦殿。并祀普贤铜像于殿中。
  同年，安徽凤阳龙兴寺僧广济，因避朱元璋之诏见和封赏，遂隐迹前牛心寺，并取西晋左思《招隐诗》句"何必丝与竹，山水有清音"之意，改寺名为清音阁，沿用至今。
- 明洪武年间，僧惠光重修普贤寺（今万年寺）。
- 明永乐十三年（1415年），僧惠光赴江西景德镇，募化瓷商塑造"卢舍那"瓷佛一尊，于当年十二月运抵峨眉县城拨云山庵（今瓷佛寺）。
- 明宣德三年（1428年），珏禅师开建普贤寺圆觉殿，铸普贤骑象一尊，并请名家绘制圆觉诸天像。
- 明成化二年（1466年），峰顶普光殿毁于火。
- 明成化七年（1471年），蜀王朱怀园捐资重建峰顶普光殿。
- 明嘉靖二年（1523年），僧大智开建净土庵于金顶大佛坪。
- 明嘉靖十三年（1534年），僧慧宗开建白龙寺于象牙坡下。
  同年，僧别传创建金顶铜瓦殿，并铸普贤像1，铜佛65尊。又开建伽蓝殿（即佛牙殿）于白水寺外，并铸铜佛3尊。
  同年冬，白水寺毁于火。
- 明嘉靖四十三年（1564年）十二月二十四日，僧别传于江阳铸造莲花铜钟3件。隆庆元年（1567年）八月十四日悬于圣积寺真境楼。
- 明嘉靖年间，卧云庵失火。金顶僧性天开建大峨寺（即福寿庵），同时复建卧云庵。
- 明隆庆元年（1567年）春，僧别传率领徒众以《法华经》字数为准，植桢楠、杉、柏69777株于白龙寺周，广袤二里，后称"古功德林"。
- 明万历二十七年（1599年）四月二十四日，明神宗朱翊钧赐《大藏经》一部置于白水寺中。入冬，白水寺毁于火。
- 明万历二十九年（1601年）春，白水寺僧台泉求募于朝廷重建寺宇。慈圣太后遂遣中贵二人携金来蜀，重建大像阁为无梁砖殿。次年九月竣工，适慈圣太后寿庆，神宗朱翊钧题"圣寿万年寺"额于砖殿之门。自此，白水寺改称万年寺，沿袭至今。

- 明万历三十年（1602年），山西五台山僧妙峰携潞安浑王朱模捐资数千来蜀，于金顶建造峨眉山普贤金殿。神宗朱翊钧题寺名"护国圣寿永延寺"。
- 明万历四十七年（1619年），四川巡抚吴用先，将其构筑于玉液泉边别墅改建为佛寺，取名圣水庵，即今神水阁。
- 明嘉靖间，无暇禅师创建雷音寺（隆庆时重修名观音堂）。
- 明崇祯十六年（1643年），僧三济开建永庆寺，亦称回龙庵。并设戒坛于庵中。
- 明崇祯十七年（1644年），伏虎寺、大峨楼、西坡寺、灵岩寺、仙峰寺毁于兵火。
- 明瑞峰禅师开建天门寺，因寺右两石对峙如天门，故名。

公元1644年～公元1839年

- 清顺治元年（1644年）秋，华严寺毁于兵燹。
  同年冬，中峰寺毁于兵燹。寺内宋时所建普贤阁，程堂所绘之《菩萨竹》壁画全为灰烬。
- 清顺治元年，僧独峰开建天庆庵（又名慧灯寺）于"五十三步"处。
  同年，僧芳海开建会佛寺于大坪岭下。
- 清顺治二年（1645年），僧闻达开建接引殿于七里坡下。
- 清顺治七年(1650年)，僧贯之建凉风桥、凉风庵(系茶庵)、"震旦第一山"坊于解脱坡下。
- 清顺治八年(1651年)春，僧贯之及其徒可闻重修伏虎寺，经时28年始成。更名"虎溪精舍"。并在寺内开建"学业禅堂"。
- 清康熙初年(1662年)，四川总督哈瞻等捐俸，令伏虎寺僧可闻重建卧云庵。
- 清康熙三年(1664年)，四川巡抚张德地率部僚捐银茸修光相寺、万年寺。并于金顶观光台处新建一坊，题名"云封雪岭"。
  同年，峨澈禅师，移建长林禅院于长老坪，俗称长老坪。
- 清康熙十一年(1672年)八月十九日，顺天府学政蒋虎臣来峨，住伏虎寺，修纂《峨眉山志》。
  同年秋，布政使金俊为蒋虎臣《峨眉山志》作序，志由壁经堂刻印。
- 清康熙三十八年(1699年)，僧行能扩建初喜亭为天花禅院，俗称洗象池。
- 清康熙四十一年(1702年)，清圣祖玄烨，赐"善觉寺"为额，以易原降龙院之名。并书"到处花为雨，行时杖出泉"为联置于寺门；又为寺住持元亨题诗，赞其德行。
  同年，玄烨题赠"报国寺"以易会宗堂之名。由承德郎(封荫)王藩书额置于寺门之上。
- 清康熙五十年(1711年)，僧峨云禅师复修卓锡庵，易名保宁寺。并重修洪椿坪、华藏、清音、仙峰诸寺。

- 清雍正年间，千佛庵僧峨云于中峰寺左侧开建观音寺。
- 清雍正七年(1729年)，僧通融于古玉皇亭旧址开建华严顶。
- 清乾隆十年(1745年)，弘历书赠千佛庵(洪椿坪)字联一幅，为："性海总涵功德水，福林常涌吉祥云。"精刻存寺，至今完好。
- 清乾隆二十六年(1761年)正月十八日，万年寺毁于火。
- 清乾隆四十一年(1776年)，僧闻奇、闻刚重修雷洞坪寺。
- 清乾隆四十三年(1778年)，大乘寺毁于火。
  同年，正月初三日，千佛禅院毁于火。
- 清乾隆四十四年(1779年)，僧玉升、泰安重建仙峰寺，僧明仙重建黑水寺。
- 清乾隆四十七年(1782年)，僧天华、真玄等重建千佛禅院(今洪椿坪)。

公元1839年～公元1912年

- 清道光二十三年(1843年)，翰林院侍读曾国藩来游，书联贻赠净土禅院。
- 清道光二十八年(1848年)，卧云庵毁于火。
- 清咸丰二年(1852年)，书法家何绍基任四川学政时来游，书苏东坡《寄黎眉州》诗句"瓦屋寒堆春后雪，峨眉翠扫雨余天"赠千佛禅院。
- 清咸丰十年(1860年)，金顶楞严阁失火，火势延及金殿、铜瓦殿、锡瓦殿等处。
- 清咸丰、同治年间，开建净水寺于万年寺下之净水溪旁。
- 清同治元年(1862年)，僧圣怀开建遇仙寺于长寿坡上。
- 清同治六年(1867年)，同治帝载淳赐《大藏经》一部，由僧明正运回，藏于金顶锡瓦殿。
  同年冬，金顶华藏寺失火，明代铸造的大峨山金殿第二次被烧，几无余存。火势延及卧云庵等处。
- 清光绪二十四年(1898年)，清宗室庆亲王爱新觉罗·奕劻来游，于万年寺书"我佛所宗，真如贝叶。众经之长，妙法莲花"一联留赠。
- 清光绪二十五年(1899年)，僧朗清扩建洗象池寺，并从杭州运回木雕"西方三圣"佛像奉于寺中，此寺遂成大寺。
- 清光绪三十一年(1905年)，遂宁县广德寺僧清福(亦名清葫)，先后两次从印度、缅甸、斯里兰卡等国迎回玉佛27尊，贝多罗叶经5部，舍利15粒，分别置于峨眉山毗卢殿、仙峰寺、普陀山南禅寺，南京居云寺等处。

公元1912年～公元1949年

- 民国4年(1915年)8月25日，洪椿坪千佛莲灯雕成。
  同年冬，金顶祖师殿失火，延及华藏寺等庙宇多处。

　　同年冬，金顶发生大火灾，烧毁华藏寺、锡瓦殿等处。
— 民国25年(1936年)初春，著名画家徐悲鸿来游，于报国寺绘《八哥新柳图》。
　　同年，著名画家齐白石来游，于报国寺写《墨芋图》。
　　同年，李济深来游，于洗象池书"即心即佛，乃圣乃神"联。
— 民国27年(1938年)4月，著名画家张大千、黄君璧来游，于接引殿合写《峨眉山水图》大中堂；黄氏于仙峰寺写浅绛山水单条两幅留赠。
— 民国28年(1939年)3月，郭沫若(时任国民政府军事委员会政治部第三厅厅长)来峨眉山。
　　同年7月23日起，国民政府主席林森寓居洪椿坪，前后达83天。
　　同年8月，四川大学为避日机空袭，迁校于峨眉山下。
— 民国30年(1941年)3月9～13日，国民政府军事委员会副委员长冯玉祥来山休假。
— 民国33年(1944年)初春，武汉大学教务长朱光潜教授来游，于洗象池题诗一幅留赠。
— 民国35年(1946年)正月初九，昆卢殿失火，延及邻近各殿，砖殿新殿幸存。
— 民国36年(1947年) 9月，刘君泽编著《峨眉伽蓝记》一书，由乐山《诚报》印刷部印行。书中记述了当时尚存73寺的历史梗概和主要文物。
— 1949年12月24日，峨眉县人民政府成立。

峨 眉 山 文 物
The Cultural Relics of Mt. Emei

后记
Postscript

凝聚着"世界文化与自然遗产"峨眉山文化精粹的大型画册《峨眉山文物》，适逢第三届世界自然遗产会议在峨眉山隆重举行之际，与读者见面了。这是峨眉山在深度挖掘文化遗产、宣传和展示峨眉山厚重历史文化所取得的一项突出成就，标志着峨眉山世界遗产保护研究迈上了新的台阶。

乐山市委宣传部长罗佳明、峨眉山风景名胜区管理委员会党委书记马元祝、主任秦福荣在百忙中为画册的编辑出版倾注了大量的心血，常务副主任冯庆川、四川省文物考古研究院院长高大伦更是亲自参与了画册从策划到编辑出版的全过程。《四川文物》编辑部曾德仁、峨眉山博物馆陈黎清、峨眉山管委会熊锋等承担了画册的协调和编辑等具体工作，文物摄影家江聪全身心地投入到文物摄影工作中。正是大家的精诚合作，使该画册能在短时间内高质量地完成编写并交付文物出版社出版发行。同时，我们还要感谢峨眉山博物馆、峨眉山佛教协会、峨眉山市文物管理所、峨眉山管委会宣传处等诸位同仁对画册拍摄工作的大力支持。清华大学教授李学勤先生欣然为画册做序，更为画册增添了几多魅力。

由于画册编辑时间短，加之我们的能力、水平限制，画册中可能存在许多不尽人意之处，还请读者见谅。

《峨眉山文物》编辑组
2007年9月于峨眉山

On the occasion of the holding of the 3rd International Conference on World Natural Heritage in Mt. Emei, highlighting the cultural essence of Mt. Emei as world's cultural and natural heritage, a large photo album, The Cultural Relics of Mt. Emei, has been published to the satisfaction of enthusiastic readers. It is an outstanding achievement in exploring in-depth the cultural heritage and publicizing and showcasing the profound history and culture of Mt. Emei, marking a higher level for Mt. Emei in the protection and research of world heritage.

Mr. Luo Jiaming, Publicity Minister of the CPC committee of Leshan City, Mr. Ma Yuanzhu and Mr. Qin Furong, the secretary and director of the CPC Committee of Emei Mountain Scenic Area Administration have taken time from their busy schedule to contribute great efforts to the compilation and publication of the photo album. Mr. Feng Qingchuan, the deputy director of Emei Mountain Scenic Area Administration Committee, and Mr. Gao Dalun, president of Sichuan Institute of Historic Relic Archaeology and Research have even taken part in person in the whole process from planning to compiling and publishing of the album.. Many other comrades e.g. Zeng Deren of the Editorial Dept. of Sichuan Cultural Relics, Chen Liqing of Mt. Emei Museum and Xiong Feng of Emei Mountain Scenic Area Administration, etc. were engaged in the coordination and editing of the book. Mr. Jiang Cong, a historic relic photographer, had been whole-heartedly involved in photographing the cultural relics. Had it not been for the dedicated cooperation of all people, the book wouldn't have been able to be published in such a short time by the Cultural Relic Press with such high quality. In the meantime, our thanks also go to many colleagues from Museum of Mt. Emei, Buddhist Association of Emeishan, Cultural Relic Administration of Emeishan City, Publicity Division of Emei Mountain Scenic Area Administration for their great support to the photo-taking of the book. It is our great delight to have Mr. Li Xueqin to contribute preface for this album, which adds some more charm to the album.

Due to the limitation of time and our capacity, there might exist some defects in this album, we hereby sincerely request in advance the generosity of forgiveness from dear readers.

Compiled by Editorial Group of
The Cultural Relics of Mt. Emei
In Emei Mountain, Sept. 2007

峨眉山文物
The Cultural Relics of Mt.Emei

装帧设计：刘　远
责任印制：梁秋卉
责任编辑：李缙云

撰　稿：
陈黎清　曾德仁　熊　锋　黄剑华　杨荣新
摄　影：
江　聪　胡晓阳　吴　健　林　萌　刘　勇
绘　图：
李建伟　彭朝蓉　王　静　宋　艳
英文翻译：
杨福雄　毛　堃

图书在版编目（CIP）数据

峨眉山文物/峨眉山风景名胜区管理委员会，峨眉山
旅游股份有限公司编著.－北京：文物出版社，2007.10
ISBN 978-7-5010-2318-9

Ⅰ.峨... Ⅱ.①峨...②峨... Ⅲ.文物-简介-中国
Ⅳ.K87

中国版本图书馆CIP数据核字（2007）第144836号

文物出版社出版发行

北京东直门内北小街2号楼
http://www.wenwu.com
E-mail:web@wenwu.com

北京圣彩虹制版印刷技术有限公司制版印刷
889×1194　1/16　印张：14.5
2007年10月第一版　2007年10月第一次印刷
ISBN 978-7-5010-2318-9

定价：320元